DATE DUE

LENIN'S EMBALMERS

*Ilya Zbarsky
& Samuel Hutchinson*

LENIN'S
EMBALMERS

*Translated from the French
by Barbara Bray*

THE HARVILL PRESS
LONDON

ibre du mausolée
997

n Great Britain 1998 by
The Harvill Press
2 Aztec Row, Berners Road
London N1 0PW

www.harvill-press.com

1 3 5 7 9 8 6 4 2

Copyright © Actes Sud, 1997
English translation copyright © The Harvill Press, 1998
Copyright © Agence Moscoop, Moscow,
for the photographs unless credited otherwise

Ilya Zbarsky and Samuel Hutchinson assert their moral right to be
identified as the authors of this work

A CIP catalogue record for this book
is available from the British Library

ISBN 1 86046 515 3

Designed and typeset in Walbaum at
Libanus Press, Marlborough, Wiltshire

Printed and bound by Butler & Tanner Ltd
at Selwood Printing, Burgess Hill

Contents

LENIN'S EMBALMERS

Lenin at Gorky in August 1923, six months before his death. Suffering from atherosclerosis, he is practically unable to speak. He has also lost his memory and can not move the right side of his body.

I

Lenin's Illness and Death

The struggle for life – and for the Party

A photograph of Lenin taken by his sister Maria in August 1923, six months before his death, shows the Bolshevik leader looking ravaged, gaunt and wild-eyed. His appearance reflects a terrible struggle with generalized atherosclerosis that had lasted nearly two years.

He had been cared for in a princely mansion in Gorky that the Soviet government had put at his disposal, but by now he had practically lost the power of speech. His right arm and leg were completely paralysed and he was prey to terrifying visions day and night. He would shriek and wave his arms about, roar with laughter for no reason, or take offence over trifles. The five doctors the Party had sent for specially from Germany he treated as enemies; he even shook his fist at Professor Förster, physician to the Krupps, the wealthy Ruhr industrialists.

It is sometimes said that Lenin's illness dated back to 1918, although medical opinion on this is still divided. At that time civil war was raging in Russia. In the elections to the Constituent Assembly in December 1917, the Revolutionary Socialists (RS) had taken 58 per cent of the 40 million votes cast, as against the Bolsheviks' 25 per cent. Lenin, therefore, believed that the only way to preserve the fruits of the October Revolution was by a forcible dissolution of Parliament. His decision touched off a powder keg with counter-revolutionary armies, foreign troops, nationalist rebels and armed gangs of looters multiplying on all sides. The situation confronting the Bolsheviks in the summer of 1918 seemed to have no solution. Their power was evaporating all the time, as was proved in July, when a wave of more active resistance to the Bolsheviks swept over Moscow. In response, the government brought in Latvian infantry and put the insurrection down.

On 30 August 1918 Lenin had just finished making a speech at the Michelson armaments factory in Moscow when Fanya Kaplan, a member of the RS, drew a gun and fired at him. The weapon, a Browning automatic pistol, was loaded with bullets dipped in curare, two of which hit her target. Striking him in the chest, one bullet shattered Lenin's shoulder blade, went through the upper part of his left lung and lodged near the junction of the right clavicle and the breastbone. No vital organs were damaged; Lenin had had a narrow escape. Even so, the doctors who performed the autopsy after his death in 1924 did not rule out the possibility that the callus formed around the bullet in the healing of the 1918 injury might have led to the atherosclerosis that Lenin developed three years later.[1]

In February 1921 the Red Army bloodily put down the naval mutiny at Kronstadt. In country regions wartime Communism, with its forcible requisitioning of harvests, provoked innumerable peasant revolts. At Tambov, south-east of Moscow, thousands of famine-struck farmers died in fighting over several months, having failed to hand over the prescribed quantities of grain on time. Everywhere there was starvation and rebellion. The Revolution was in danger of collapsing.

On 15 March, at the Tenth Congress of the Communist Party of the Soviet Union (CPSU), Lenin announced a crucial change to the political programme: the "New Economic Policy" (NEP). This ended requisitioning, introduced some taxation in kind, and permitted private trading by allowing the peasants to sell their surpluses, a freedom which did much to restore the country's commerce.

It was then that Lenin, worn out by the effort he had put into the Revolution, experienced the first symptoms of illness, suffering from acute headaches and insomnia. Towards the end of 1921, the migraines grew worse, and he decided to take his doctors' advice and go to Gorky to rest. After a few days there, he was working again, but on 22 May 1922 he suffered his first stroke: he lost consciousness for a while, his speech was impaired, and his right arm and leg were partially paralysed. From then until October he took no part in political life. Yet even though he had some speech difficulties, his intellectual powers were unaffected. By the end of August he was back in harness, and in October he presided over the Sovnarkom, the Council of People's Commissars. According to contemporary accounts, however, he was greatly changed: very frail in appearance, he was also less lively and incisive as a speaker. It proved to be his last public appearance.[2]

By December 1922 Lenin was having daily attacks. He knew that these presaged the end, and, forced to give up political activity for ever, he used his remaining strength to warn those about him of the dangers which threatened Russia. Of these, what he feared most of all was the fierce struggle between Stalin and Trotsky for the succession. In his *Letter to Congress*[3] of

5

Leon Trotsky.

December 1922, better known *as Lenin's Testament*, he set out his own appraisal of the two men. In his view, Stalin "has concentrated in his own hands a vast amount of power, and I am not sure he always knows how to use it wisely." As for Trotsky, while Lenin refers to his "exceptional abilities", he also considers that he "is too self-confident" and "rather too prone to look at things from the purely administrative point of view". Haunted by the risks of division within the Party, however, Lenin was careful not to designate an official successor.

A few days later, on 4 January 1923, after a quarrel between his wife, Nadezhda Krupskaya, and Stalin during which the latter had behaved particularly roughly, Lenin added a note to his "will". "Stalin is too uncouth," he wrote, "and while we Communists may be prepared to put up with this shortcoming among ourselves it is not tolerable in someone acting as General Secretary. I therefore suggest my comrades should consider how Stalin may be removed from that post."

It was already too late, however. On 24 December Stalin had sent for Lenin's doctors, Professors Kojevnikov, Kramer and Ossipov, and ordered them to forbid their patient all further visitors or any other communication with the outside world,

Stalin visits Lenin in Gorky, August or September 1922.

though he did allow him to dictate his thoughts to a stenographer for five or ten minutes a day.[4] Then, on 10 March, Lenin suffered another stroke, as a result of which he lost the power of speech.

According to the autopsy performed after his death, "Narrowing of the arteries impeded the flow of blood to the brain, the left part of which – the area controlling memory and speech – was partially destroyed." Such words as he uttered were incoherent, his memory was confused, and he suffered extreme agitation. Nevertheless, watched over by his wife, the only person whose presence did not irritate him beyond endurance, he attempted some speech therapy. His determination was remarkable, and by August he was able to recite as many as three hundred and fifty words.

Yet thus imprisoned within himself, Lenin was forced to look on helplessly as Stalin and Trotsky battled for the succession. It was a war waged against a background of two crucial national problems: economic policy and the rapid disappearance of every vestige of democracy within the Communist Party.

The NEP had resulted in a disparity between industrial and agricultural prices that left the proletariat much worse off. By 1923 industrial prices had risen to between 189 and 200 per cent of their pre-war levels, while agricultural prices had increased by only 50 per cent. In order to curb inflation in the industrial sector the government ordered a reduction in expenditure, which in turn resulted in a number of business mergers and a rise in unemployment. The number of people without work increased from 500,000 to 1,300,000 in less than a year; wages stagnated while prices continued to mount. Trotsky rebelled against this "sacrifice of the working classes", and against the rise of the "Nepmen", the nouveaux riches who had feathered their nests under the NEP. In his view, the growth of even more glaring inequalities could be avoided only by a radical reform of the economy based on rapid industrial development and an overall economic plan.

Trotsky was not to prevail, however, for the right of the Party, represented by the troika of Stalin, Zinoviev and Kamenev, insisted that the NEP must continue. They maintained that the policy had brought about an economic renaissance: Russia's agricultural production was approaching its pre-war level; industry was beginning to function again; people were returning to the cities, many of which had been all but deserted during the years of the Civil War. To the troika and their supporters, only compromise with the farmers could produce an agricultural market strong enough to provide industry with the capital it needed. Since this point of view was still shared by most senior members of the Party, Trotsky and his adherents found themselves in the minority. The NEP remained.

On 18 October 1923, Lenin went to Moscow for the last time, travelling in a car driven very slowly, its tyres filled with sand to make the ride as smooth as possible. Inside the Kremlin, he made for the chamber of the Council of People's Commissars, his paralysed right leg forcing him to walk slowly, leaning on a stick. When he reached his office he searched through the drawers of his desk, but in vain. According to one of his biographers, N.V. Valentinov-Volsky, "He thought he would be able to find papers damaging to Stalin. But Stalin had discovered that such documents existed and taken steps to have them removed. Lenin was so upset his symptoms immediately grew worse again."[5]

By now his condition had become so alarming that the question of the preparations for his funeral began to be considered.

9

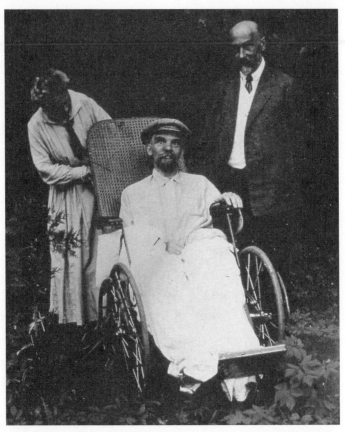

Lenin, his sister Maria and Professor Förster at Gorky in 1923. His intense, if weird, stare contrasts with his weak physical condition. Lenin was fighting against his illness but, imprisoned within himself, he could only look on helplessly as Stalin and Trotsky battled for power.

Valentinov-Volsky tells us that Stalin took it upon himself to summon a meeting, held behind closed doors, of the Politburo, at which he was the first to moot the idea of embalming Lenin's body.

Held in late October 1923, the secret conference was attended by six of the eleven members of the Politburo: Trotsky, Bukharin, Kamenev, Kalinin, Stalin and Rykov. No minutes of the meeting exist; no decision was recorded. All that is certain – at least, according to Bukharin – is that these discussions took place some time after Lenin's last visit to the Kremlin on 19 October 1923.

That day Stalin is supposed to have said: "Comrades, Vladimir Ilich's health has grown so much worse lately that it is to be feared he will soon be no more. We must therefore consider what is to be done when that great sorrow befalls us. I understand our comrades in the provinces are exercised about this matter. They believe that it is unthinkable that Lenin, as a Russian, should be cremated. Some of them suggest that modern science is capable of preserving his body for a considerable time, long enough at least for us to grow used to the idea of his being no longer among us."

To this Trotsky angrily replied: "If I understand Comrade Stalin correctly, he proposes to replace the relics of Saint Sergei Radonezhsky and Saint Serafim Sarovsky with the remains of Vladimir Ilich. This is what, to judge by his lengthy and obscure remarks, he seems to be driving at in his reference to what is and is not fitting for 'a Russian'. I myself should very much like to know who these 'comrades in the provinces' are who imagine that science is capable of preserving Vladimir Ilich's body. I should like to tell them that they have learnt absolutely nothing about Marxist dialectic."

"Trotsky is right," said Bukharin. "To turn Lenin's remains into a relic would be an insult to his memory. We should not even contemplate such a thing." Kamenev agreed with Trotsky and Bukharin: "There are other equally effective ways of honouring his name. For instance, to remind people of the role he

Josef Stalin.

played in the October Revolution we could change the name of Petrograd to Leningrad. Or we could print millions of copies of his works. But the embalming idea strikes me as reminiscent of the very 'priest-mongering" that Ilich himself denounced in his philosophical writings."

The indignation of Trotsky, Bukharin and Kamenev left Stalin unmoved, however. He was careful not to name the "comrades in the provinces" who wanted to embalm Lenin, for the simple reason that this had been his own idea: he saw it as a good way of harnessing the religious sentiment of the ignorant masses in order to ensure the survival of the regime. Again according to Bukharin, Stalin knew that in due course he could count on the support of the other, absent, members of the Politburo and of most of those who made up the Party apparatus.

Trotsky, having been thwarted over changes to the economic policy, launched another bid against Stalin, this time on a purely political plane. On 8 October he publicly denounced the complete lack of democracy within the Party. In particular, he objected to the fact that Felix Dzerzhinsky, the chief of the political police, OGPU,[6] had suggested in June to the CPSU sub-committee on internal affairs that all members of the Party should have to report to OGPU any anti-government or otherwise divisive activities that came to their notice. This was tantamount to turning every Party member into an informer.

On 15 October Trotsky and forty-six Party members whose support he had won wrote to the Politburo demanding that it call a meeting of the Party to discuss both the dictatorial methods prevailing within its own ranks, and the disastrous results of the New Economic Policy. On the 27th, however, at a plenary session of the Central Committee, Stalin won approval for a vote condemning Trotsky and the forty-six other signatories for divisive activities endangering the unity of the Party. Stalin had won a decisive point in a battle for dominance which, by 1929, would leave him in sole power.

He had picked his time well, for Lenin's health continued to deteriorate. Nearly four months later, on 20 January 1924, he seemed to be trying to tell his doctors that he could no longer see, though Professor Averbach, a celebrated oculist, could detect no deterioration in his vision. At six in the evening of the following day, however, Lenin was seized with violent convulsions. His breathing grew more and more irregular and his pulse rate rose to 130 beats a minute. At six-thirty the pulse slowed down, the patient's state resembling that of an epileptic emerging from a fit. His temperature rose to 42.3 degrees C, and at six-fifty he suffered a stroke. His face turned red, and for a moment he seemed to be trying to sit up. Then suddenly he stopped breathing. His head fell back and his face turned deathly pale. The autopsy established that he "died from cardio-respiratory arrest following a brain haemorrhage in a context of atherosclerosis".

There is a bizarre postscript to this bizarre end. For a long time after Lenin's death rumour had it that he had suffered from creeping paralysis brought on by syphilis. The doctors who performed the autopsy, however, categorically denied this in an appendix to their report: "No sign of syphilis was found in the analysis of the blood, or of the brain and spinal fluids, or in the results of the autopsy."[7] Nevertheless, Bunin and Shulgin, two emigrant Russian writers, have maintained the opposite view, as have other commentators. It is true that the treatment Lenin received, based on the administration of iodine, mercury, arsenic and bismuth, was almost indistinguishable from the remedies then used to deal with "la maladie honteuse". Yet so politicized are opinions on this sensitive question that even today it is impossible to decide the truth of the rumours.

II

The Prehistory of the Mausoleum

Should the body be frozen or "balsamed"?

"Comrades, workers and farmers, men and women, I have an important request to make of you. Do not let your sorrow be transformed into demonstrations of adoration for Vladimir Ilich's personality. Do not put up buildings or monuments in his name. When he was alive he set little store by such things; indeed, he actively disliked them.

"You know the poverty and disorder that afflict our country. If you want to honour Vladimir Ilich's memory, build crèches, kindergartens, houses, schools and hospitals. Better still, live according to his teaching."[8]

The exhortations of Lenin's widow, Nadezhda Krupskaya, which were published in *Pravda* on 29 January 1924, went unheeded, however. The "cult of Lenin" was inaugurated immediately after his death. The Party laid on a grandiose funeral; Petrograd was renamed Leningrad. Moreover, the idea of preserving Lenin's body, first aired by Stalin at the secret meeting of the Politburo in late October 1923, began to be seriously debated.

Before long it had turned into an affair of state. If the archives

Gorky, 22 January 1924. Lenin on his deathbed surrounded by workers and peasants. Nadezhda Krupskaya, his widow, is at far left.

of the Russian Centre for the Preservation and Study of Contemporary Historical Documents (CRCEDHC) are to be believed, it was Dzerzhinsky who was responsible for actually launching the project. On the evening of 23 January, during a meeting of the committee responsible for organizing the funeral, the head of the political police declared: "Kings are embalmed because they are kings. In my opinion, the question is not so much if we should preserve Vladimir Ilich's body but how."[9]

On 26 January *Izvestiya* recorded that "in accordance with the wishes expressed by many workers and peasants, the Presidium of the Central Executive Committee of the USSR has decided on the long-term preservation of Vladimir Ilich's body."[10] The archives of the Lenin Institute, however, show that the Politburo decided on the embalming on the evening of Lenin's death – that is, before the alleged "wishes of the workers" had had time to be uttered. The episode is a good illustration of what the Bolsheviks meant by the "dictatorship of the proletariat": the pretence that a suggestion had originated with the rank and file, whereas in fact the matter had already been decided by the Party leadership.

Another episode was to leave a lasting mark on the practices of Soviet power, which would come to accord enormous significance to the observance of protocol at the funerals of the country's heads of state. From the time of Lenin's funeral, it has been possible to tell, from the order of precedence among the guests and from the presence or otherwise of Soviet notables at such ceremonies, which officials are in favourable positions in the struggle for power.

Thus on 27 January 1924, according to the procedure laid

Lenin's remains lying in state in the Hall of Pillars in the House of Trade Unions, Moscow. Beside him, some leaders of the USSR. Centre (with beard): Felix Dzerzhinsky, head of the OGPU; second and third from right: Abraham Belenky, head of Lenin's guard; and Kliment Voroshilov, a high-ranking commander in the Red Army and member of the Central Committee. The hall would later be used for show trials during the purges of the 1930s, and later still for the lying-in-state of Stalin's body.

down by the Politburo, Stalin and Zinoviev were to be the chief pallbearers when Lenin's coffin was carried from the Hall of Pillars in the House of Trade Unions, where it had been lying in state, to Red Square. Trotsky, significantly, happened to be staying by the Black Sea at the time, apparently recovering from a mysterious illness. The funeral was originally scheduled for Saturday, 26 January,[11] which effectively left Trotsky unable to return to Moscow in time to take part. Even though the ceremony was ultimately postponed to the Sunday, Stalin decided not to inform Trotsky of this, preferring that his rival should not be present at this highly symbolic occasion. So it came about that at four in the afternoon of Sunday, 27 January 1924, after the leaders had made their speeches, Stalin, Zinoviev, Kamenev, Molotov,

The long queue of Russians waiting to pay their last respects to the founding father of the USSR as he lay in state in the Hall of Pillars. Lenin's body was displayed over four days, from 23 January 1924 until the state funeral on 27 January.

Stalin, Bukharin, Kamenev and Zinoviev carrying Lenin's coffin into the temporary mausoleum. The presence of these leaders already heralded their future high position within the regime. Trotsky was deliberately kept away from the ceremony.

Bukharin, Rudzutak, Tomsky and Dzerzhinsky carried the coffin of the first Soviet leader to a plinth inside the mausoleum that had been prepared for it.[12]

Three days earlier the Kremlin had decided to build a temporary structure to house Lenin's corpse, and a team of Red Army soldiers had been ordered to use explosive charges to blast a suitable hole in ground hardened by a frost of minus 30 degrees C. By the 27th "temporary mausoleum", as historians have called it, was ready. This was a sort of shed built of grey-painted wood and surmounted by the name "LENIN" carved in Cyrillic capitals. Visitors entering by a door on the right of the building saw the body in the middle of the room, lying in its open coffin in a grave three metres deep.

January 1924. It took three days, in temperatures of minus 30 degrees, to build this first wooden mausoleum, known as the "temporary mausoleum". The Red Army soldiers charged with its construction had to use explosives to dig into the frozen ground.

Lenin's name in Cyrillic capitals on the temporary mausoleum decorated with a wreath. In front of it lay graphs and slogans, symbols of the Communist economic success.

The corpse was, however, already showing the first signs of decomposition: the skin of the face and hands had darkened, wrinkles could be seen on various parts of the body, and observers noted that the lips had become slightly parted. This evidence of decay set the Soviet authorities off on a race against time. A "committee of three", made up of the Bolshevik leaders Molotov, Yenukidze and Krasin, tried frantically to find a way of saving the corpse from decomposing.

Krasin, a former engineer with no specific qualification in biology, was the first to come up with a solution: refrigeration.[13] The "committee of three" therefore ordered a series of tests to be carried out on corpses, although even before the results of these tests were known they ordered refrigerating equipment from abroad. Meanwhile Professor Vorobiov, head of the anatomy department at Kharkov University in the Ukraine, learned of statements in the press by doctors whom the "committee" had consulted, in which they declared that the long-term conservation of a dead body was an impossibility.[14]

"It is hard to believe", Vorobiov protested, "that anyone could talk such rubbish! In my own laboratories I have anatomical specimens that are thirty years old and in a state of perfect preservation." His remarks were reported to Zhuk, then head of the medical training department in the Ukraine, who urged Vorobiov to inform the Moscow authorities of his experiments.

The professor was dubious, however: he knew how dangerous it would be for him if he failed. He politely declined Zhuk's suggestion, saying success would depend on being able to work under the best possible conditions, and these, he was sure, would never be made available to him.

Shrugging off these objections, Zhuk reported his conversation with Vorobiov to Zatonsky, People's Commissar for Education in the Ukraine, who immediately dispatched a telegram to Dzerzhinsky in which he declared that the Ukraine had the honour – indeed, the privilege – of employing an outstanding expert on embalming in the person of Professor Vorobiov. "I may add," Zatonsky concluded, "that Vorobiov guarantees the success of his method."[15] Learning that Zatonsky had approached Dzerzhinsky, Vorobiov's colleagues now did their best to persuade the professor to put his skill at the service of the country. Still Vorobiov dragged his heels. But when he received a telegram from Dzerzhinsky requesting that he come to Moscow forthwith, he could hesitate no longer.

While all this was going on, Krasin still clung to his idea of refrigeration, to which end he tried to win support from eminent physicians and biochemists. Early in February he paid a visit to one of the latter – Boris Ilich Zbarsky. And so it was that my father came to be involved in the debate about the embalming of Lenin's body.

I do not know how Krasin came to be in touch with my father, nor whether this had anything to do with the fact that the latter was then Assistant Director of the Institute of Biochemistry, nor even whether the two men had met before. The answers to these and other questions are probably to be found in the book on the embalming of Lenin that my father wrote after the Second World War. Unfortunately, however, the book is still kept secret in the archives of the mausoleum laboratory, with the result that I have never been able to read it. All I can do, therefore, is refer to the work of Yuri Lopukhin,[16] a laboratory assistant who has had access to my father's account.

Krasin told my father about the idea of freezing the body,

and immediately received the reply that this would not prevent decomposition. On the contrary, refrigeration destroys cells and may therefore accelerate autolysis.[17] Furthermore, from a practical point of view it would be very difficult to maintain a constant low temperature around the corpse. And even if these problems could be solved, the glass of the sarcophagus would be bound to cause condensation and damp. Krasin brushed these objections aside: "Once the body is frozen and the tissues 'fixed' with formalin," he said, "the enzymes causing autolysis will become inactive. As for the sarcophagus, leave that to me. A system of double glazing will eliminate condensation." Not wishing to offend a senior Bolshevik, my father kept silent. Even so, that conversation acted on him as a kind of catalyst. As he was to write later: "From then on I was obsessed by the idea of becoming involved in the preservation of Lenin's body. And naturally I thought of Vorobiov as the man best qualified to find a long-term solution."

For his part, Vorobiov arrived in Moscow on 28 February, and was met in Red Square by Krasin and Professor Abrikosov, a well-known anatomical pathologist who, immediately after Lenin's death, had been asked to carry out an autopsy on his body and then embalm it. As soon as Vorobiov entered the temporary mausoleum he could see the corpse was in poor shape. Not wishing to fall foul of such an influential figure as Abrikosov, however, he congratulated him on "having managed to keep the body in such satisfactory condition for over a month". Certainly Abrikosov's methods had been somewhat primitive. He had injected a solution of formalin, alcohol and glycerine into the aorta, but some of this fluid had leaked out of the body, and the process of desiccation seemed to be taking its course unchecked.

On 5 March there was a meeting of the "Committee for

the Immortalization of Lenin's Memory", presided over by Dzerzhinsky. This too marked the first appearance of another enduring aspect of Soviet power: its mistrust of men of science, coupled with the tendency of Communist leaders to interfere in purely scientific matters. This attitude was to be seen in an even more acute form in the 1940s, at the time when the baleful influence of the Soviet plant biologist Lysenko was at its height (pp.145–56).

At the meeting, a discussion ensued between the scientists and the politicians about the best way of preserving Lenin's body. Krasin, backed by Dzerzhinsky and Molotov, stuck to his idea of refrigeration. Vorobiov ventured to observe that "this solution might well accelerate the process of deterioration already begun." He also took the opportunity to point out that although Lenin's body had been brought from Gorky to Moscow when the temperature was minus 30 degrees, so that refrigeration had effectively already started then, this had not precluded certain disturbing developments: the nose had darkened, the eyes had sunk in their sockets, and there were brown marks round the skull where it had been sawn open to extract the brain. It should be noted in passing that Lenin's brain was already being studied in a research institute charged with demonstrating that the father of the Revolution had been a "genius". Vorobiov had no doubt that the only viable method of preserving Lenin's body was to immerse it in a liquid containing glycerine and potassium acetate.

The politicians thought little of this idea, however. Molotov declared that the refrigeration method – "the most realistic" – ought to be examined by a scientific sub-committee consisting of People's Health Commissar Semachko and Professors Weissbrod and Rozanov, to which Krasin angrily objected that "Semachko hasn't a clue and only the Committee for Immortalization is qualified to decide." Whereupon Professor Savielev, head of the laboratory of the Red Army administration, put forward a third solution, suggesting that the body be preserved in nitrogen. Not surprisingly, Krasin came down on this like a ton of bricks. "Out of the question!" cried the veteran Bolshevik. "Nitrogen wouldn't prevent the appearance of anaerobic microbes. But refrigeration at minus 6 degrees would rule out bacteria altogether." In answer, Vorobiov merely commented that "enzymes continue to function even at low temperatures".

Once their opinions had been heard, the scientists were asked to withdraw, for only the politicians were empowered to take decisions. Dzerzhinsky was the first to give his verdict. He rejected out of hand Vorobiov's suggestion that the body be immersed in the balsamic liquid, nor did he even bother to give his reasons. As for refrigeration, he wanted to seek the advice of foreign experts. Krasin intervened again. "We're not going to ask everyone in the world to give an opinion!" he said. "It's for us alone to decide."[18] Yenukidze and Molotov were more cautious, however, and agreed with Dzerzhinsky that foreign specialists should be consulted.

On the evening of 11 March, while G.V. Schorr, a professor of thanatology in Leningrad, was dining at home, he was surprised to hear a muffled knocking at the door. "Who is it?" he called. "Open up," came a man's voice. "That's an order. We're from the OGPU." Schorr turned pale, convinced that the secret police had come to arrest him.

When he opened the door three men in black leather coats burst into the room. They ordered him to pack his bags and then escorted him to a special coach on the Leningrad-Moscow train. During the journey the professor envisaged the worst: forced "confessions" of crimes he hadn't committed, exile in Siberia; perhaps even summary execution. His imagination working overtime, he began to wonder whether he was the innocent victim of a denunciation by some colleague or neighbour.

It was with considerable amazement that he learned on his arrival that he was going to be interviewed by Dzerzhinsky himself. What Schorr did not know was that a few days earlier a sub-committee of scientists had expressed an interest in his method of preserving anatomical specimens by steeping them in glycerine and acetate, fixing them in formalin, and then storing them in hermetically sealed containers.

The professor, however, dashed the hopes of his fellow scientists by explaining that his method could be applied only to certain parts of the body, such as the head or the arms and legs. Moreover, each organ had to be treated separately and kept immersed in its own container, something that was obviously out of the question in this case. Schorr's caution was, however, probably also due to dread of taking on the awesome responsibility of embalming Lenin. He went on to say that he was against immersion, while refrigeration struck him as the worst option of all: low temperatures, he too pointed out, would not eliminate the action of the enzymes.

The results of the refrigeration tests carried out on dead bodies were to prove him right. Freezing had a damaging effect on the tissues. As Professor Vorobiov had foreseen, patches of wrinkles and an ominous reddening appeared after only a few days. This irrefutable evidence did not, however, stop Krasin getting his way at a meeting of the Central Committee of the Party on 14 March, when it was unanimously agreed that the refrigeration method be adopted.[19]

While he was in Moscow Vorobiov stayed with my father, whom he had met on a trip to Berlin. During the war, the Germans, who had occupied the Ukraine, had forced Vorobiov to sign a letter saying that the Bolsheviks had killed most of the people found dead in a Kharkov suburb. He then emigrated to Bulgaria, where he taught at Sofia University. After the October Revolution, it would have been dangerous for him to return to the USSR, for he was regarded there as a sort of traitor. He was eventually allowed to back in safety thanks to my father, who interceded with the Soviet authorities. Vorobiov was, however, still afraid of being arrested, and he did not want to get involved in as politically delicate an under-taking as embalming Lenin. My father now did all he could to persuade him to accept. "Please put that idea out of your head," his guest replied. "If you get mixed up in this business it will be the end of you. As for me, I don't want to suffer the fate of the alchemists who undertook to embalm Pope Alexander VI – they had themselves paid a great deal of money but they were so inept that they destroyed the body and had to flee for their lives." "Why did you come to Moscow, then?" asked my father. "I was sent for. I had no say in the matter." He wanted, Vorobiov added, to go back to Kharkov as soon as possible. He was sure Krasin's idea of refrigerating the body would result in a fiasco, and he wanted nothing to do with it. My father, however, would not give up, and therefore conceived an elaborate plan. To begin with, he persuaded Vorobiov to write a letter addressed to, but actually dictated by, himself, Professor Zbarsky. "I leave for home," wrote Vorobiov, "convinced that the discussion will drag on for a long time yet, but that nothing will be done to save the body, despite

27

the fact that the face is already losing its colour. A few more days and it will be quite black and wizened. It goes without saying that it cannot be shown to the public in such a state." My father was later to recount how this letter had to be dragged out of Vorobiov word by word. Even so, the latter had a good deal of confidence in his friend, and had no inkling of his audacious scheme.

My father next persuaded Vorobiov to write another letter, this time to Krasin, setting out his position: "Esteemed Leonid Borisovich, since I am about to leave Moscow I consider it my duty to inform you once again of my opinion. The state of the body is worsening by the day. The drying-up process, and the consequent wrinkling of the tissues, which struck me at once when I first examined the body, is proceeding virtually before our eyes. The only way of halting the decomposition is, I repeat, by immersing the body in balsamic liquid."[20]

On 12 March, Vorobiov left Moscow for Kharkov. Only a few days later, however, Krasin went to see him there, and he was taken to see the professor's remarkable collection of anatomical specimens: a large lecture room in which were shelves laden with jars containing human organs; these, in spite of having been kept for several years, were in an exceptionally fine state of preservation. Krasin was astonished at how closely they resembled living organs. He handed Vorobiov a letter from Dzerzhinsky. "The Committee [for Immortalization]," wrote the head of the OGPU, "requests you to take such measures as you think necessary to preserve Vladimir Ilich's body."[21] Vorobiov could not believe his eyes.

What had happened? What was the explanation for the committee's sudden change of mind? On 13 March, the day after Vorobiov left Moscow to return to Kharkov, my father had decided to approach Dzerzhinsky himself, for he planned to use Vorobiov's letters as a direct offer to undertake the embalming. He began by going to see Piotr Bogdanov, Chairman of the Russian Higher Economic Council, whom he knew well; Bogdanov spoke to Dzerzhinsky on the telephone, and the latter agreed to the meeting.

My father, having worked out beforehand how best to handle the interview, began by asking if it had been decided that Lenin should be buried. Dzerzhinsky's answer was evasive. But my father was not going to beat about the bush. "We are ready to save the body," he declared. "Who's we?" came the reply. "Vorobiov and myself." Dzerzhinsky looked at him doubtfully, and remarked: "At last, some people ready to commit themselves and take a few risks." My father then handed over the letter which, at his dictation, Vorobiov had written to him.

Dzerzhinsky, clearly disarmed by this display of effrontery, said that he could not take such a decision on his own and would have to put the offer to the government. Nevertheless, he thought that it had some chance of being accepted; however, Krasin would also have to be consulted. He rang him up and asked him to see Professor Zbarsky right away. Krasin, infuriated by a last-minute interference that threatened his own plans, received my father standing up, not even offering to shake his hand. "What are you and Vorobiov up to?" he demanded. "He's a weakling who makes no practical suggestions of his own but just criticizes other people's. What is it you're proposing?" My father replied that even if he and Vorobiov were to fail, the body could be buried sooner or later.

It was true, as Krasin knew, that the corpse had by now

Lenin's body in the vault of the temporary mausoleum before it was properly embalmed. From left to right: Professor Vorobiov, leader of the embalming team; Abraham Belenky, head of Lenin's guard; and Benjamin Guerson, Dzerzhinsky's secretary.

deteriorated still further. The lips were now three millimetres apart; there were more brown patches on the thighs; the left hand was turning a greenish-grey colour; the ears had crumpled up completely.[22] "What do you really want of me?" Krasin demanded angrily. "I don't want anything," replied my father. "It was Dzerzhinsky who sent me." Yet even before he received the green light from the chief of the political police, Zbarsky phoned Vorobiov in Kharkhov and said, "It's all settled – there's no turning back now." "In that case," groaned the other, "you and I are both lost."

The government, having learned that the refrigeration tests had proved a complete failure, finally accepted my father's offer. Krasin therefore had no choice but to take the train to Kharkov again to try to smooth things over with Vorobiov. The professor soon gave the government his answer. "I consider," he wrote reluctantly to Dzerzhinsky, "that the offer made to me by the government is both an honour and a chance for me to discharge a debt. Work must begin without further delay."

Back in Moscow once more, Vorobiov was given carte blanche on all the points he specified: the mausoleum was to be closed to the public throughout the four months the work was scheduled to take; he was to be given all the technical support he required; and he was to choose for himself the people he wanted to work with.[23] Among these was Boris Ilich Zbarsky.

And so, two months after Lenin's death, Vorobiov and his assistants were at last able to start work on the embalming. They were all well aware of the enormous responsibility they were taking on. They knew, too, that the slightest mistake might cost them their lives.

III

My Father

A scientist with ambition

After the October Revolution many intellectuals and scientists refused to work with the Soviet authorities. Whether they were Revolutionary Socialists, liberals or monarchists, most of them preferred to emigrate to Europe rather than live under the "dictatorship of the proletariat".

My father thought differently, however. He believed that he had everything to gain from the new order. Being Jewish, he had suffered greatly in his youth from the harsh restrictions imposed on his co-religionists by the Tsarist regime. Although he had degrees from the universities of both Geneva and St Petersburg, as a Jew he was barred from applying for a post in any public body, and thus had no chance of making a career either in a university or in any of the highly esteemed scientific institutes.

For him, therefore, as for many other Jews, the October Revolution was a kind of revenge against the old system. He had been particularly outraged by the way Jews without higher education had been forced to live in regions like Byelorussia, Lithuania and part of the Ukraine. But what he had hated most were the pogroms, clandestinely organized at regular intervals by the Tsarist authorities to exploit the anti-Semitism of a Russian people resentful of the rigours imposed on them by the war.

It was not surprising, therefore, that some Jewish intellectuals were among those most determined to destroy Tsarist power. In 1917, no fewer than eight of the twenty-one members of the Central Committee of the Bolshevik Party were Jews, including such illustrious names as Sverdlov, Kamenev, Zinoviev and Trotsky.

The other reason why my father espoused the new government's ideas was that as a youth he himself had taken part in revolutionary activities. Born in 1885 in Kamenetz-Podolsk, a county town some forty kilometres from the Austro-Hungarian frontier, he had become a Revolutionary Socialist at the age of sixteen. The RS advocated individual terrorism as a method of fighting the established order – a method that had already claimed the lives of leading members of the state apparatus such as the Mayor of Moscow, Grand Duke Sergei Alexandrovich, and Plehve, a Minister of the Interior. Tsar Alexander II had suffered a similar fate at the hands of a Nihilist group.

My father's political persuasions were, however, rather surprising in the light of his social origins. His mother came from a family of well-to-do merchants, and had opened a china shop of her own which brought her in a comfortable income. By contrast, his father, though of distinguished aristocratic lineage, worked as a lowly clerk in an insurance company. Yet this background was no hindrance to their son, who loathed Tsarist Russia, then a country in which the gap between rich and poor was wider than anywhere else in Europe. Thus when an RS official called Gerchuny suggested he should help smuggle newspapers, books and revolutionaries across the frontier, my father agreed to the idea with enthusiasm, although he was still at high school at the time. One of the revolutionaries he helped to flee abroad, he told me, was Leon Trotsky, whom he took one night to a hut a few kilometres from the frontier. They were awakened the next morning by the curses of a smuggler, come to escort the fugitive to Austria-Hungary.

In 1967, when I was in France on a scientific mission, I met some Soviet compatriots in a Paris hotel. One of them was a philosopher, there to instruct the local communists in Marxism-Leninism. The informers in our delegation being temporarily absent, he advised me to go to the Bibliothèque Nationale to read the works of Trotsky, which had for many years been banned in the USSR. Taking his advice, I asked at the library to see Trotsky's *My Life*, and very instructive I found it. The book tells how, fleeing from exile in Siberia, Trotsky crossed Russia and after a month on the run found himself in Kamenetz-Podolsk, where a schoolboy was supposed to arrange for him to cross the frontier. The youth, however, refused at first to help him, saying that he disapproved of the Social Democrat party, of which Trotsky was one of the leading members. The Social Democrats rejected individual terrorism, advocating an uprising of the working classes against the ruling regime as the best means of rising to power. It took the brilliant theorist of the revolution three hours to overcome the resistance of this wrong-headed youth, who – as Trotsky also noted in his book – had since become an eminent Soviet scientist. He was careful not to mention his name, so as not to get him into trouble. Reading *My Life* I realized how much my father had embellished this episode, although I didn't hold it against him, knowing that under Stalin it had been almost impossible not to misrepresent historical facts.[24]

News of the schoolboy's revolutionary activities eventually

My father, Boris Ilich Zbarsky, in 1910, when he was still studying chemistry at the University of Geneva. He had been forced to emigrate to Switzerland after being expelled from school for revolutionary activities.

leaked out, and my father was expelled from his school and obliged to continue his education abroad. In 1906 he went to the University of Geneva, where for five years he studied chemistry in the faculty of physics and mathematics. As his Swiss degree was not recognized by the Russian government he had to sit a series of further examinations at the University of St Petersburg in order to gain the equivalent qualification. He then worked for a year and a half as Professor of Biological and Analytical Chemistry at Moscow University, although without receiving any salary. As the Tsar's regime forbade any Jew to occupy a public post, he had to give private lessons in maths, chemistry and physics so as to support his young family as best he could.

My father and mother, who had known each other since they

My mother, Faina Nikolaevna Zbarsky, shortly after her marriage to my father in 1908. She was also a student in Geneva.

were children, had married in 1908 when they were both students in Geneva. My father adored my mother then. She was what is often described as a "Jewish beauty", having regular features, large dark almond-shaped eyes, chestnut hair with glints of bronze, and a slim waist. But, as my father realized later, she was also rather simple-minded. As a student she had got no further than her third year in biology. Me she tended to regard as a sort of toy, and, when all is said and done, she took little notice of me. She had wanted a daughter but in 1913 gave birth to a son, which perhaps explains why she dressed me in girl's clothes, something which caused me a good deal of grief.

Not long after my birth our circumstances were to change dramatically, however. In June 1915 a young man in servant's livery arrived unexpectedly at my father's flat and asked him to go as fast as he could to see Zinaïda Grigorievna, widow of Savva Morozov, one of the wealthiest men in Russia. "She'll offer you a wonderful job," said the young man, "Don't hesitate!"

My father, who liked the unexpected, obeyed without asking for explanations. Out in the street a carriage drawn by two horses stood waiting, and in this he was driven to a large mansion in Spiridonovka Street (now used for official functions by the Foreign Ministry). Inside, waiting for him at the top of a grand double staircase, was an extremely beautiful woman. She was fair, with long legs, a broad round face, an ivory complexion, full lips, high cheekbones and ice-blue eyes – a classical Russian type. She looked my father up and down. "Are you a chemist?" she asked. "I have degrees from the Universities of Geneva and St Petersburg," he answered. "I like you. You've got the job," said Zinaïda Grigorievna.

This was perhaps typical, for she was a very capricious woman.

After Morozov's death she had married Rezvoy, the Mayor of Moscow, and they were joint owners of the Gorky estate where Lenin was to die nearly nine years later. Her orders had to be carried out immediately, even though she might change her mind a few minutes later; any employee who did not obey instantly was automatically dismissed. On hearing that her estate in the Urals, which included two chemical works, was not bringing her any profits and that her steward was embezzling large sums of money, she had sacked him at once and given her butler an hour to find a replacement. Panic-stricken, he had picked up a newspaper, where his eye lighted on a small advertisement that read: "Boris Zbarsky, Doctor of Chemistry, Universities of Geneva and St Petersburg, gives private lessons in chemistry, physics and mathematics." It was the butler who had hurried round to our house.

Zinaïda Grigorievna offered my father a salary of 500 roubles a month plus 5 per cent of the income from the estate, Vsevolodo-Vilva, which consisted of the two chemical factories and some forty hectares of forest. Five hundred roubles! It was more money than my father had ever dared to imagine. Even so, he to had to weigh the advantages and disadvantages for a moment: a job like this would be bound to keep him from his scientific research. In the end, however, he accepted Zinaïda Grigorievna's offer, not least because my mother had been urging him to get a job, any job so long as he was paid for it.

Thus, in 1915, began our new life in the Urals. I was then two years old, and my earliest memories date from that time. I can still see myself playing with a couple of dogs bigger than I was – Damka, a russet-coloured bitch, and the dark Valetka; walking round the snow-covered yard of our house with my *niania* (nurse); or running to meet my father as he came home from work. That was the most important moment of my day. I liked to run in and out between his legs, apparently a favourite form of amusement with me; indeed my father once found me trying the same trick with a horse, and risked a kicking himself to haul me out by the scruff of the neck.

My parents and I were happy in Vsevolodo-Vilva. Our standard of living had improved considerably: we lived in a twelve-roomed house with a coachman, a cook, a chambermaid, my *niania*, and a man to tend the stoves, all at our permanent disposal. I remember going for magnificent walks when spring came round, seeing the bluish peaks of the Ural Mountains, the rush of the rivers when the snow melted, the summer meadows covered with flowers. Although Russia was heavily engaged in the war, we practically never heard any of the grim news from the Eastern Front. Moreover, as the director of a chemical works regarded as vital to national defence, my father was exempt from conscription.

Even so my mother, with her husband at work all day, was lonely. As a result, my father decided to invite his friend, the writer Yevgeny Lundberg, to come and keep her company, something to which Lundberg willingly agreed. Then one day when he was in Moscow, my father ran into Boris, the son of his friend Leonid Pasternak, the painter. They got into conversation, and Boris complained of the crowded conditions in which he and his family lived, and which hampered him in his work. My father therefore asked him, too, to be his guest in the Urals. A few days later Boris Pasternak, whom at that time my father scarcely knew, joined us in Vsevolodo-Vilva, and thus a small circle of intellectuals gathered on Zinaïda Grigorievna's estate.

My father, busy at the factory, took only a minor part in these

Vsevolodo-Vilva, Zinaïda Grigorievna's estate in the Urals, 1915. Boris Pasternak, my niania *(nurse) and me. The young Boris Pasternak, as talented a musician as he was a poet, stayed with us for a long time.*

activities. Boris Pasternak, then just twenty-five, played the piano and wrote poetry. His mother was a very good pianist and a friend of the composer Scriabin who, recognizing the young Boris's talent, had encouraged him to take up music as a career.

In the Urals, 1915. From left to right: Yevgeny Lundberg, my father, my mother, and Boris Pasternak. A small circle of intellectuals less serene than it appeared. While my father was busy at the factory, Pasternak passionately courted my mother.

Pasternak, however, had not yet made up his mind whether to be a musician or a poet.

He used to recite his verse to Lundberg and my mother. He had fallen in love with her, and apparently she was not indifferent to him; to this day I still have some verses he dedicated to her. Some were scribbled down on scraps of paper, others were typed on official Vsevolodo-Vilva headed paper, with its line that read "Suppliers of acetic limes, acetone, various grades of methyl alcohol, chloroform and charcoal." Some of these verses were published, among them this:

> Over dinner, screwing up your eyes,
> Through the facets of the cut glass
> You could follow the progress
> Of phalanxes of passionate ideas.

They were an emulsion
Of days kept in the depths of the heart,
And you were the final convulsion
The last drop.

A chilly morn. Our teeth were clenched
And the stir of the leaves was like a frenzy.
Bluer than the plumage of wild ducks
Day broke sparkling on the far bank of the Kama.

And morning, in the bloodbath
Of a sunrise spreading like oil,
Would douse the lamps in the officers' mess
And the streetlights in the towns.

> *Vsevolodo-Vilva*
> *17 May 1916*

Others, however, have never been published:

That day all of you, from your combs to your feet,
Like a provincial actor with a Shakespearian tragedy
I carried you about in me and knew you by heart,
Wandering round the town rehearsing you.

The sun rather weighs me down during the day,
Congealing like wax on a pewter plate,
But night – a nightingale – engulfs the day
And the house turns into an Aeolian harp.

Often, my mother and Boris Pasternak would sing together or
play duets on the piano. My grandmother, who had come upon

them doing so, used to say to my father: "What! Can't you see she's in love with him? It's obvious!" I was too young then to be able to say whether her suspicions were justified. Nevertheless, it is not impossible that the relationship between Boris and my mother might have helped to worsen the situation between her and my father.

A tall, lanky fellow always deep in thought, Boris Pasternak was certainly a strange character. Once, many years later, I met and greeted him on the Bridge of Stones in Moscow. He failed to recognize me at first, seeming to be in a dream from which he emerged only with difficulty. The first syllables he uttered were incomprehensible; then, "Oh, it's you!" he said, showing his large, horsy teeth in a smile.

He walked with a limp, which until 1916 allowed him to avoid conscription. By then, however, the war effort was drawing in everyone, even those who were partially handicapped, and he knew that he was bound to be called up sooner or later. But my father managed to get him a job in the Bondjusky chemicals factory, whose work was deemed indispensable to the national defence, with the result that young Boris escaped having to go to the front.

On the estate at Vsevolodo-Vilva my father had been horrified by the way the factory workers, mostly Tatars, were treated, and not least by the way they were swindled on paydays. The wages clerk always arrived with a case full of hundred-rouble notes. Since the men's wages were mostly less than ten roubles or so – a derisory amount even in those days – the large notes had to be changed into smaller ones, which gave the local moneylenders the chance to levy large commissions. This gave rise to all kinds of disputes, and my father insisted that the wages clerk should come supplied with notes of smaller denominations. He got his way in the end.

He was even more outraged by the medieval conditions in which his employees lived, cooped up in insanitary wooden huts without running water. He moved them to another, disused factory, and had the old huts burned down. For this, however, he was immediately sent for by the regional governor, who informed him that what he had done amounted to an act of insubordination towards the government. He now found himself in a tricky situation. With the intensification of the war the wind seemed to turn in his favour, however. The governor summoned my father for the second time. The Tsar had just released a new manifesto addressed to all chemical plant directors: Russia urgently needed various chemical products formerly imported from Germany, among them medicinal chloroform, which was regarded as essential. My father, helped by his assistant, J.V. Filipovitch, devised a new and improved method of producing and purifying chloroform, and his invention was immediately adopted by the military authorities. He took out a patent, and was ordered to organize production in Russia. He then contacted his friend, L.Y. Karpov, a chemical engineer in charge of the Bondjusky factories near the Kama river. Together they created a chloroform department there, and my father was appointed head of the factory's laboratory. As a result, we all moved to Bondjusky, Yevgeny Lundberg and Boris Pasternak electing to come with us. In 1917, after the February Revolution, Professor Alexei Bach, my father's former teacher in Geneva, returned from exile and joined us. As a Revolutionary Socialist Bach had been persecuted by the Okhrana (the Tsarist political police), and it is true that he did supply explosives to extremists bent on eliminating members of the Imperial family and of the Tsarist establishment. He had emigrated to Switzerland, where he had run a private biochemistry laboratory. It was he who had supervised my father's thesis when he was a young student at the University of Geneva, and after the October Revolution my father did all he could to enable Bach to return to Russia.

In 1917 my father was elected RS deputy for Elabuga, although his enthusiasm for the October Revolution soon waned when, after the elections for the Constituent Assembly, the RS became one of the chief targets of the new regime. Then Karpov, who was a Bolshevik, was placed in charge of all the chemical industry in Russia. He suggested that both Professor Bach and my father should come to Moscow because a new chemistry laboratory was being set up there. As a result we all moved back to the capital in early 1918, only to face difficult times once again. No decision had been made yet regarding the laboratory and the Civil War was raging. Moreover, my father had to wait before he was able to find a job.

My memories now become clearer. I can still see the room – divided up by a wardrobe – in which my father, my mother and myself were all crowded together. The Pasternaks lived on the floor above, and sometimes we would have dinner with them. They seemed a very patriarchal group, with the painter Leonid Pasternak at the head of the table, flanked by his sons, Boris the poet and Alexander the architect. At the other end of the table sat his wife, the pianist Rosalia Isidorovna, and his two daughters, Josephine and Lydia. They were a very united family, although they were to split up under the pressure of later events: the parents and the two daughters emigrated first to Berlin and then, after the rise of Hitler, to England, while the two sons chose to stay in Russia.

I was five years old, and my father made me learn our address by heart in case I got lost: "Volkhonka, house number 14." One day when we were out for a walk along the boulevards, he carried out an "experiment", suddenly hiding. Left alone, I started to cry. After a while he reappeared, but instead of comforting me he scolded me for not going up to a passer-by and telling him where I lived. This was unfair of him, I think: I was too small; moreover, ever since then I have been afraid of being abandoned. It is said that childhood is the happiest time of one's life, but for me it was the most difficult. What I remember are the cold, the constant hunger, the water coming through the ceiling, the puddles on the floor, my

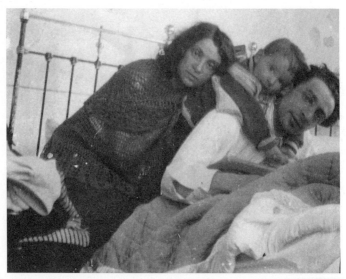

My mother, my father and me back in Moscow in 1918, during the years of hardship. Since we lived in a small room in which we were constantly cold, we used to huddle together to keep warm.

46

parents' quarrels and, later, the divorce. There seemed to be no way out, although I was nevertheless consoled by the hope of a better future.

One day in the spring of 1918, staring out of our window, I saw some rough-looking workers and students hauling on cables to pull down the huge bronze statue of Tsar Alexander III seated on his throne. Later, in the summer, I heard the sound of firing close at hand. My father closed the shutters and told me to stay away from the window. This, as I found out later, was the day – 6 July 1918 – on which the Bolsheviks bloodily put down the revolt of the left-wing RS.

Soon after these events some men in leather coats burst into our room, shoved me out of the way, and began to search through all our things, throwing my beloved books on the floor. They proved to be agents of the Cheka (the forerunner of the OGPU). As they could find nothing compromising they had to let my father go, but we were obliged to move to an even smaller room in Great Nikolo-Vorobyinski Alley. The place was draughty, bitterly cold in any wind, and when it rained so much water came in through the ceiling that we were up to our ankles in it – I used to walk on the chairs to keep my feet dry. When autumn came we wrapped ourselves in blankets and huddled together for warmth.

As the country sank deeper into civil war, food grew scarcer and scarcer in the cities. We ate anything we could get hold of – mouldy potatoes, stale bread – and drank an infusion of lime-tree flowers instead of tea. I remember being so hungry one day that I bit into a greyish-brown object that looked like a bread roll, only to find it was a lump of soap.

My parents, instead of facing these difficulties together,

quarrelled all the time. There were hysterical scenes, much yelling and broken china. To shield me from such distressing scenes, my father would tell me to go out for a walk, but I was still so afraid of being alone that I preferred to wait outside the door until I was allowed in again. I don't know what caused those endless rows, and I was in any case too young to understand. My parents finally thought it best to send me to stay with my aunt. I was there for more than a year.

By this time my father's professional status had suddenly become less uncertain. Professor Bach had been appointed Director of the Institute of Biochemistry, newly founded by the Soviet authorities, and my father, then aged thirty-six, became chief assistant. This was a considerable promotion for both of them, although it was partly explained by the fact that many experts who had occupied key positions under the Tsarist regime refused to work with the current government, thus leaving the way open for a new generation of scientists.

Once more our standard of living greatly improved. We now lived in a large three-roomed apartment, part of the mansion that had become the new Institute of Biochemistry. Here we were surrounded by beautiful furniture and fine carpets, pictures and statuettes. The house had belonged to a German industrialist named Mark who had left Russia in such haste after the October Revolution that he had not been able to take all his possessions with him. The servants, too, had been left behind, so that the Institute inherited a staff of eight that included a caretaker, a gardener, a cook, a butler and a chambermaid.

In front of the house the grounds stretched down to the river Yaouza. The garden had suffered a great deal during the years of revolution and was overgrown with weeds and briars, although here and there we could still see traces of former splendour: a grove of limes, rows of fruit trees, a dried-up lake crossed by a little wooden bridge. Because of the food shortages we grew potatoes and turnips in the kitchen garden, and sometimes, digging them up, I would unearth rifles, pistols and machine-gun ammunition, doubtless buried by fighters in the Civil War.

My father, although very taken up with his scientific work, paid more attention to me than did my mother, even though she was not working at the time. He used to tell me stories and explain natural phenomena to me. Even so, as I grew older he began to put more and more pressure on me, an authoritarianism which became so extreme that, as we shall see, I was eventually left with no freedom at all.

Meanwhile relations between my parents became increasingly violent, and on some evenings my father did not even come home to the flat in Vorontsovo-Polé Street to which we had just moved. Officially he was working day and night in the labora-tory, but for all I know he may have been with some mistress. By the beginning of the 1920s my parents were no longer living as man and wife. After they separated my mother, needing a job, started work in a hospital laboratory. She found a room in a communal flat, although as she was still having finan-cial problems, my father carried on supporting her. One result of all this was that they decided that I would stay with him, because his flat was bigger and I could have my own room there.

In 1921 I was enrolled at the local school. I can still remember my first day there. All the pupils in my class were singing the "Internationale", but as I had never heard it before I didn't join in. Suddenly the teacher burst into the room and told the children to "Stop singing Yid tunes!" At breaktime some of them, having noticed I had not taken part in the singing, beat me up. When I got home my father, seeing my glum looks, asked me what was wrong. I didn't tell him about the fight. He was, however, taken aback when I asked him what a "Yid tune" was. After this he decided to take me away from the school – he had in any case a poor opinion of state education, believing lessons at home to be more effective. So between the ages of eleven and thirteen I had three tutors, one for mathematics, another for history and a third for German. Since I was at home all the time, however, I missed the sort of company I would have had at school, and for which I envied other children.

Going down the stairs one day when I was nine years old, I passed a man I had not seen before. Aged about forty and sporting a moustache, this was Professor Vladimir Vorobiov, just arrived from Berlin. He had no difficulty making a friend of me, for he gave me an orange. I had never seen one before, though by this time Russia was gradually recovering from the great privations of 1919 and 1920. Lenin's New Economic Policy was just beginning to show results, and fruit, vegetables, meat and bread started to reappear on people's tables. At last I actually had enough to eat. These were good times for my father and me. Grusha, a maid who had been on the staff of the previous owner of the house, cooked and washed for me and kept my room tidy. When friends came to see me she would serve us tea and cakes.

My father – slim, possessed of a quick intelligence and a proud bearing, and always dressed in an impeccably tailored three-piece suit – cut a fine figure, and one that seemed to appeal to women. After he and my mother parted he had many mistresses. I took a great liking to one in particular, a tall, fair-haired, bright-eyed actress and singer called Olga Baklanova, prima donna in the Stanislavsk-Nemirovich-Danchenko Musical Theatre, who had had a particular success as Carmen in Bizet's opera. My father had a passionate affair with her; indeed, he came very close to marrying her, though in the end she decided to go and live in the United States. It was probably through her that he came to know Ozerov, the singer, and Moskvin, an actor at the Art Theatre, both of whom used to come to our house for dinners washed down with plenty of wine.

Moving as he now did in theatrical circles, my father was eventually made a member of the artistic committee of the Musical Theatre. I once attended one of its meetings, and remember how keenly its members deplored the lack of realism in some of the music of Lev Knipper, a then fashionable composer who was a nephew of Olga Knipper-Chekhovna, wife of the great playwright Anton Chekhov.

Under the NEP the arts continued to enjoy a good deal of freedom. It was not until the late 1920s that the regime began increasingly to inflict the dreary canons of "socialist realism" on the public. In the years before then, however, French operettas like Offenbach's *La Belle Hélène* and *La Périchole*, and Lecocq's *La Fille de Madame Angot*, were all the rage in Moscow. These were lively shows with exotic sets and costumes, often with plots about amorous intrigues that did not at the time mean much to me.

In 1923 my father and I went on a long trip round Europe. This was an unusual thing to do in those days, but the devaluation of the rouble had made foreign travel feasible. In Berlin I was struck by the clean and orderly streets, in marked contrast to the dirt and chaos of Moscow. Almost everywhere I could hear people speaking Russian, for several million of our compatriots had fled Russia after the Revolution, and hundreds of thousands of them had emigrated to Germany. Among them were Leonid Pasternak and his wife and two daughters, whom we went to see. I remember a lively meal during which my father defended the new Soviet regime tooth and nail against the caustic criticisms of our hosts.

I heard a lot of Russian in Paris, too, for thousands of emigrés had settled there. Though we stayed only two days I was greatly attracted by the bustle of the streets and the exuberance of the French, a far cry from the severity and monotony of Berlin. From Paris we went to Cherbourg and there embarked for the Spanish port of Vigo, where my father's brother lived; he too had fled Russia. On our arrival the first thing that caught my eye were the orange-sellers, oranges being practically unobtainable in Russia. The women selling them jostled around the boats, hoisting their wares up to the ship's decks on ropes running through pulleys. When a passenger accidentally dropped an orange, one of the women yelled out "Bolshevik!" – this being, apparently, the worst possible insult in Europe then.

On we went to Madrid, Barcelona, Genoa, Florence and Venice, where I was greatly impressed by the beauty of the canals, the ancient bridges and the gondolas. I have to admit, however, that I remember very little about that journey through post-war Europe. I was then not yet ten years old, and it was not until many years later that I realized how lucky I was to have been able to leave the USSR. Apart from professional trips to Berlin in 1945 and to Sofia in 1949, I had to wait until I was forty-seven before I was allowed to travel abroad regularly.

After a spell of intense work during which he sometimes did not come home at all, the second half of 1924 brought my father a period of prosperity. He used to take me shopping to buy handsome suits for us both. It was then, too, that he began to give grand

At the Institute of Biochemistry in 1924, the year Vorobiov and my father embalmed Lenin. From left to right: Vorobiov, my father, and me. As a child, I had become very fond of Vorobiov, who was always friendly towards me.

dinners at our apartment. I was unaware of the reasons for this affluence, but years later he told me that for his work on Lenin's body he had been paid 25,000 roubles, a considerable sum under the Communist regime.

During the three more years that the NEP lasted, my father lived – and entertained – in great style. Most of his dinner guests were senior officials in the government or the police, although I do not know what made him choose to associate with such people. Perhaps he was trying to establish durable relationships with people who might turn out to be useful to him. Whatever his reasons, however, the embalming of Lenin had catapulted him into the higher echelons of power.

IV

School Years

A privileged family

As I have said, my father had made the acquaintance of Felix Dzerzhinsky at the time when the embalming of Lenin was being resolved. He remembered how helpful Dzerzhinsky had been to himself and Professor Vorobiov during the work, and used to refer to the founder of the Soviet political police as "a remarkable man who has done a great deal for our country". One day Dzerzhinsky gave him a signed portrait of himself, and my father lost no time hanging it up in our drawing room; indeed, he admired the man so much that he named his second son Felix. Even after Dzerzhinsky's death in 1926, my father maintained excellent relations with his deputy, Genrikh Yagoda.

One day in 1927, during the time when the NEP was at its last gasp, Yagoda sent for my father and handed him a large black box that had been found a few days earlier outside OGPU head-quarters, and asked him to analyse its contents. It contained a considerable quantity of melinite, an explosive so powerful it could have destroyed the whole building. According to the news-papers, the person responsible for this failed attack was a man called Operput, an OGPU employee of Latvian origin working for

Felix Dzerzhinsky, head of the OGPU, who gave Vorobiov and my father the task of embalming Lenin, although not without a little underhand lobbying on my father's part.

an underground organization led by a high-ranking princess. In short, Operput was a double agent. When he was unmasked he fled, seizing a revolver with which he held up a car, forcing the driver to take him out of the capital. After a few kilometres, however, the car ran out of petrol. The fugitive took to the woods but was soon caught by OGPU officers. Operput was executed and the princess's network dismantled.

The fact that the OGPU asked my father to analyse the explosive showed how much confidence the secret police had in him. Certainly he did all he could to get on close terms with those in power. Naturally ambitious, and with a passion for money and decorations, he believed that such people might advance his career.

As soon as he started working at the mausoleum our family became part of the nomenklatura of the new regime. At the age of thirteen, therefore, I was enrolled at a high school where many of the pupils were the children of leading members of the Party or the government. "The Lepechinsky Communal College, Moscow" (MOPCHK), was its official name, but it was nicknamed "the school for lapdogs" (*mops* in Russian). It was a big, grey, three-storey building in the Ostojenka district, right in the middle of Moscow. Among its pupils were the daughter of Rykov, Chairman of the Sovnarkom, the Council of People's Commissars; Felix Dzerzhinsky's son; and Vassily, son of Stalin. I was in a higher class than Vassily, so I never had any direct contact with him, but I remember a red-haired boy with a reputation for being a swine. Every time a teacher asked him a question in class he would thump the desk and say "I'm Stalin!" The teacher, duly intimidated, would pass on to the next pupil.

One day, in 1928, we were all urgently summoned to assemble

in the yard, where one of the masters walked up and down in front of us and told us that Stalin was now head of the Party. He made a long speech about Stalin's life and his part in the Revolution; "He is Lenin's best disciple," he declared. Stalin had just emerged victorious from a struggle between himself and the left of the Party apparatus led by Trotsky who, although he had been expelled from the Politburo in 1927 and exiled to Central Asia, continued to repeat Lenin's warnings against Stalin, and to condemn the latter's naked ambition. Stalin had violently opposed Lenin's policies, in particular his ideas on economic planning and the militarization of labour; subsequently, however, the wily Georgian took over those policies in order to rid himself of the right of the Party as represented by Kamenev and Zinoviev.

All channels of information – press, radio, hoardings, propaganda in schools and factories – were now under Stalin's control. In 1929 *Pravda* published an editorial by the General Secretary of the Party entitled "The Year of the Great Watershed", proclaiming the forcible industrialization of the country and the collectivization of the land – "necessary stages in our progress towards the bright future that is Communism". The progress promised by these measures soon took the form of famine, however, and Russia sank into a new period of privation.

Our school was not exempt from the ideological bombardment. The teachers never stopped dinning it into us that "the Great October Revolution" had freed Russia from the terrible exploitation of the bourgeoisie and had brought happiness to all the workers. On religious holidays we were made to demonstrate outside the Cathedral of Christ the Saviour[25] carrying anti-clerical banners which read "Down with the priests! Religion is the opium of the people."

This indoctrination also had repercussions for our school curriculum. Russian language and grammar were abolished in favour of "social sciences", and we were taught that history began with Karl Marx and the First International. Anything which happened before that was held not to have existed. Literature lessons dealt chiefly with works by proletarian authors. One book by someone called Gladkov, evocatively titled *Cement*, described the lives of workers in a factory in the Northern Caucasus not far from the Black Sea port of Novorossiisk. The hero, a contagiously enthusiastic member of the Party, urged his colleagues to do their best to reach the targets set by the Five-Year Plan, and castigated those workers who were too fond of the bottle. Another – *Torrent of Iron* by Serafimovich – depicted a practical hero of the Civil War ready to give his life for the revolution. We also studied the verses of Demian Biedny ("Demian the Poor"), the poet of "socialist realism" who spared no effort to win the favours of the regime, although before the Revolution he had written an ode to Nicholas II:

> I sound my lyre
> I write my song
> To Nicholas II, apostle of peace.

Once he dedicated a poem to the physicist Gamov, whose researches had caused a great stir at a foreign symposium:

> He's a Soviet lad
> Who's showed those bourgeois scientists
> That he's cleverer than they.

In penning these inspired lines, Demian the Poor could not have foreseen that the scientist in question, while attending a conference in Paris some time later, would ask the French government for political asylum. From then on Gamov's name in Russia was anathema.[26]

Sometimes, however, we were allowed to read a few poems by great writers such as Brisussov and Blok, though never anything by Esenin, Gumiliov, Akhmatova or Sologub, while most of Dostoevsky was also officially banned.

Our school was a pilot project meant to test a new educational method imported from the United States in the 1920s. According to the "Dalton Plan", as it was called, pupils were meant to work on their own, within a group but without a teacher present. Those lessons when we were left alone to ask one another questions with the aid of a book were, however, simply good opportunities for all kinds of mischief. We made water-bombs and threw them down on to the passers-by, or used phosphorus from the chemistry lab to write our names in luminous letters inside a cupboard door. One day the headmaster called us into his office to tell us that the cupboard had caught fire. He read us the riot act at great length.

Our teachers' job, according to the authorities, was to make us "understand working-class reality". One result of this was that our chemistry teacher took us on a month's tour of factories in the Ukraine. During this trip I was very impressed by the colossal size of the foundries in Zaporojie, where workers in rags, their faces streaming with sweat, poured huge crucibles of molten metal into small trucks. In the Donbass (the Donets Basin, the industrial and coal-mining region of the eastern Ukraine) we saw miners hacking at the coalface in cramped galleries reeking of gas. Apparently the lives of the workers were as wretched as ever, despite all the slogans about the great improvement in their conditions. For me, though, the outcome of this journey was that on our return to Moscow I gave a lecture on the chemistry of metallurgical processes.

Official attempts to introduce new teaching methods in Russia were still very tentative. Despite the Dalton Plan our teachers, most of whose careers had begun before 1917, continued to use the methods in force in the Tsar's time. On the whole, however, they gave us a solid grounding, especially in the natural sciences. Thanks to my chemistry master I made an early acquaintance with the principles of qualitative and quantitative analysis. We specialized in our last two years, and I left high school in 1930 with a certificate in chemistry.

Meanwhile my father continued his social rise. He was now married to Eugenie, whom he had met in Berlin, at the Pasternaks' (she was a friend of one of their daughters). He had fallen in love with her immediately. I have never understood why – she was a headstrong woman, with a mean and petty nature. When she came to Moscow he made her head of research at the Institute of Biochemistry, though she was completely unqualified for the post.

My father liked cultivating links with leaders of the regime. Among others, he had got to know Alexei Rykov, who after Lenin's death succeeded him as Chairman of Sovnarkom, the Council of People's Commissars. While this had made him in essence a kind of prime minister, his authority was largely sapped by Stalin who, as General Secretary of the Party, concentrated all power in his own hands.

Rykov invited my father, my stepmother and myself to go for a holiday to his dacha (country house or cottage) at Valuevo, about twenty kilometres from Moscow. The place, which once had belonged to Count Mussin-Pushkin, was a two-storey house made of logs, with ten or so rooms modestly furnished with beds, oak tables and cane chairs. Facing the house was a pinewood enclosed by a fence and leading down to a river, where Rykov, my father and I used to bathe. The whole setup was closely guarded by a Latvian officer and a Russian soldier.

A second, smaller dacha on the same estate was inhabited by another senior member of the Party – Nikolai Bukharin, editor of *Pravda*. This brilliant theoretician of the Revolution was responsible for questions of ideology within the Politburo, but as an avowed supporter of the NEP he too had been marginalized by Stalin.

Bukharin often came to see us. He was about forty and, with his small moustache and goatee and his razor-sharp intelligence, he struck me as a kind of "musketeer of Bolshevism". His knowledge was encyclopedic, and he could talk with equal ease about politics, economics, literature, zoology and botany. I remember how one day, as we were going down to the river, he gave me a detailed explanation of all the different kinds of plants we came across in our walk.

Rykov was more reserved. Tall, with a carefully trimmed beard and always wearing a dark suit, he had the bearing of a head of state. Sometimes, however, he would take off his jacket and scythe the grass in the meadows, and occasionally he would even indulge in a few jokes. At a meal with us one day he announced that the Minister of Agriculture's real name was Epstein, not Yakovlev. "Oh, comrade," cried my Jewish stepmother, "you're an anti-Semite!" "Excuse me, madame," replied the Chairman of Sovnarkom, "it's not me who's an anti-Semite – it's him, for changing his name." We all laughed except my stepmother, who pulled a face.

In the evenings we would all gather in the dining room for supper, and I remember that neither Bukharin nor Rykov made any bones about criticizing Stalin's policies; "He's presiding over the degeneration of the nation," I heard Rykov say once. Both men were opposed to the collectivization of farms, which had led to the extermination on a large scale of the kulaks, the better-off peasants who owned their own farms. Rykov, Bukharin and another leading member of the Party were soon accused of "right-wing deviationism", and were later to pay a heavy price for their opposition to Stalin.

As it happened, both Rykov and Bukharin were proved right. It was not long before the repercussions of the policy known, in the then current jargon, as "liquidation of the kulaks as class enemies" began to be felt throughout the country. Once again I knew what it was to go hungry. The strange thing was that my father went on eating his fill, having lunch in the canteen of the Kremlin Hospital, and in the evening, after work, collecting provisions from the secret network of shops reserved for members of the nomenklatura. The OGPU let him have coupons that allowed him to bring home fruit, vegetables, cheese and ham – all practically unavailable to the rest of the population. Eugenie, my stepmother, would grab the parcels of food, and stow them away in a larder with a double lock. Later she would cook splendid meals for my father which I was never invited to share.

It has to be said that Eugenie displayed towards me a cruelty and a meanness bordering on the incredible. Once she went to Palestine and brought back a crate of oranges, which were still very hard to come by in Russia. It never even occurred to her to give me one, although when by chance I came across the crate a few months later I saw that all the remaining fruit had gone mouldy. On the very first day she crossed our threshold she summarily dismissed our chambermaid, Grusha, who loved and cared for me. Nor was starving me enough for her; she had to steal my clothes as well, although I still cannot understand what she could have done with them. I seldom told my father about these harassments, however. No doubt my pride prevented me, but in any case, Eugenie was very good at turning him against me.

My only comfort in those days was Professor Vorobiov. After Lenin had been embalmed he returned to his chair at the University of Kharkov, but twice a week he would come to Moscow to attend to his duties at the mausoleum. Every time he visited us I realized how much he meant to me. He was very sociable, and seemed to regard me as an equal. With him at least I felt free, not awkward and constrained as I did in the presence of my father and other grown-ups. My father apparently resented my feelings for Vorobiov. "If I'm more reserved with you," he said to me one day, "it's because I love you more. I want you to be properly brought up."

Vorobiov enjoyed the pleasures of life, especially the theatre and the company of pretty women. He often took me out to dinner at a restaurant – a great treat, given the privations I suffered at home. He was a connoisseur of wine, and spoke very knowledgeably about the effects of different vintages on the palate, the sort of glasses they should be drunk from, and so on. Sometimes he would arrive in Moscow accompanied by a typist. "You know my weaknesses," he would say to me with a meaning look.

At other times he would speak to me about Lenin's corpse. He told me about the various histological preparations used, and about how tissues could be embalmed in gelatine or artificial

Professor Vorobiov in 1934, three years before his mysterious death. Dedicated to science, he wasn't interested in society events, preferring to devote his spare time to indulging in pretty women and good wines.

resin. I must admit that I was not terribly interested, for I knew nothing at all about the subject then.

In the course of one of our conversations the professor asked me what I intended to do when I grew up. I said I wanted to be a biochemist. "It's important not only to study chemical processes themselves," he told me, "but also to understand them in the context of tissues and cells." The study of cellular nuclei was still largely unknown territory, though progress in biochemistry was

ИНСТИТУТ МАРКСА – ЭНГЕЛЬСА – ЛЕНИНА при ЦК ВКП(6)

Проф. Б.И. ЗБАРСКИЙ

МАВЗОЛЕЙ ЛЕНИНА

ОГИЗ · ГОСПОЛИТИЗДАТ · 1944

A copy of The Lenin Mausoleum, *the booklet my father wrote. The print run totalled nearly 300,000 copies, and after its publication in 1944, he came to be regarded by the public as Lenin's principal embalmer.*

later to show how important a field of research it was. Even so, Vorobiov's advice was to be a great influence on my future career.

Unlike my father, he made no attempt to curry favour with officials of the regime. True, he benefited from his involvement with the embalming of Lenin's corpse (a fee of 50,000 roubles and a private apartment), but he seemed to take little pride in that. All he was interested in was science and the teaching of science.

In 1944, seven years after Vorobiov's death, my father wrote a booklet called *The Lenin Mausoleum*. After it was published – it ran into two further editions and a total print run of nearly 300,000 copies – the public tended to associate the embalming of Lenin with the name of Zbarsky alone. The part played by Vorobiov faded into the background. This was to some extent an injustice, for the long-term preservation of Lenin's body had been achieved through the use of Vorobiov's methods. It seemed to me that my father, who had no previous experience in that field, had somewhat exaggerated his own role.

V

University Years

"Students who are socially useful and students who are not"

In January 1934, on the tenth anniversary of Lenin's death, the authorities decided to bring some younger scientists into the team responsible for preserving the body. As a result, Vorobiov and my father suggested that I should work with them in the mausoleum, although the idea didn't appeal to me much at first. During my years at the university I had been more interested in pure, rather than applied science: conducting experiments on corpses did not, therefore, strike me as a very attractive career.

The beginning of my university career in 1931 had coincided with a definite ideological hardening of the regime. Any activity that fell outside the limits prescribed by the Party was frowned on. Intellectuals were by definition "bourgeois". Clearly, where the state was concerned, it was necessary to create a "new class of intellectuals" as soon as possible. Only the children of workers and peasants were to be considered worthy of higher education, however. I managed to enter the university only because of the Order of the Red Flag of Labour awarded to my father for his work on Lenin's corpse since, from the state's point of view, this award was the equivalent of "working-class origins".

I remember my father taking me one day to a meeting of the Medical Institute where the subject of "purging" professors was on the agenda. In the course of the meeting these academics were supposed to prove the "purity" of their social origins and their unconditional devotion to the Party. Everybody, students and minor employees included, had the right to question and criticize them. It was thus that the "socially useful" students ruled out the professors who were not "socially useful". Naturally, those members of the teaching staff who awarded the lowest grades in examinations were the first victims.

As a result, when I entered the chemistry department of Moscow University it was at a time when higher education was in a state of utter chaos and upheaval. I discovered at once that the faculty in which I'd enrolled was soon to be transformed into an Institute of Chemistry, charged with producing experts useful to the socialist economy. Subjects like organic and physical chemistry were doomed, for the new institute was supposed to train engineers to produce sulphuric acid, polymers, aniline dyes, and so on. My own idea, however, was to improve my knowledge of chemistry. "Our country doesn't need chemists," I was told curtly. I could not help thinking of the judge who sentenced Antoine Lavoisier to death during the French Revolution. When someone pointed out that Lavoisier was a great scholar, the judged replied, without batting an eyelid, "The Republic has no need of scholars".

Meanwhile, throughout Russia, heads were rolling. The papers printed column after column denouncing "saboteurs" guilty of every iniquity under the sun. In 1928 there had been staged the great trial known as the "Shakty Affair", which ended in the conviction of fifty-three engineers from the Donetz coalmines.

They were accused of sabotage carried out on behalf of "a committee of merchants and industrialists" consisting of former landowners who had emigrated to France. Eleven of those convicted were shot by firing squad.

Another and even more sensational trial took place late in 1930. The chief prosecutor alleged that an "industrial party" run by the French General Staff had established branches all over the USSR. Its aim – or so the state said – was to restore capitalism through the combined intervention of the imperialist powers.

In the meantime, my own trials continued at the university. As there was no chemistry department I decided to enrol for biology. To my considerable disappointment, however, I learned that the biology department no longer existed, and that only those of botany and zoology had survived. Here too I was thwarted, for biology, physiology and zoology had all been removed from the curriculum, since these subjects had also been judged of no use in the construction of a socialist state. Zoology, for example, was now called "the science of hunting"; entomology was "the battle against parasites"; ichthyology "the fishmongering industry"; and so on. The sole remaining department that appealed to me was that of "physical and chemical biology". Since this was the only one the Party had not yet managed to blight, I decided to join it.

Military training, however, ranked first and foremost in the university education offered to us. Consequently all the male students in our department, some three hundred in all, were ordered to report to a camp in the suburbs of Moscow. Most of the youths belonged to the "class of up-and-coming intellectuals" of which the regime had such need. They had not been able to enter the highly regarded department of mechanical engineering because they were not good enough at maths. Indeed, most of them had had almost no secondary education; some couldn't even sign their own names.

Once we had finished our military training I discovered that even the subject of physical and chemical biology had been dropped. I had to fall back on the department of "work physiology", although I was relieved to learn that here at least the fundamental sciences of maths, chemistry and physics were still taught. Two-fifths of the curriculum, however, was taken up by politically oriented subjects such as the history of the Party, political economy, the economics of socialism, historical materialism, dialectical materialism and the dialectics of nature. I loathed all these subjects. One day when I was being examined on historical materialism the Rector of Moscow University asked me what part German social democracy had played in Hitler's rise to power. I answered that the Social Democrats had done nothing to oppose it, and was duly failed. What I should have said was, "The Social Democrats actively helped the fascists come to power."

For years, the authorities had given priority to institutes of technical education, with the result that the universities, relegated to a secondary position, did not even have enough funding to keep their premises in good repair. Our department, located in an old Moscow University building dating from the early nineteenth century, was no exception. The classroom floors were covered with dust, the grimy white walls were peeling, festoons of cobwebs hung from the ceiling, and the heating system did not work properly, so that in winter we had to muffle ourselves up in thick woollen jumpers. One day our class was suddenly plunged in darkness, and as the university had no spare bulbs I took it upon myself to fetch one from a light in the adjoining room. We then went on with our work, but a quarter of an hour later the professor of comparative anatomy rushed in, shouting, "A fine thing, I must say! So now students of Moscow University steal light bulbs!" Fortunately for me, as no one said anything the professor just turned on his heel and stormed out again, banging the door behind him.

If the physical discomfort we suffered was great, so too was the intellectual, for there seemed no limit to the brainwashing we were subjected to. Three times a week we had to teach the history of the Party to junior office staff, while another chore was compulsory attendance at interminable meetings of the Konsomol. As a schoolboy I had dreamed of being a "konsomol"[27] not least because we were always being told that members of communist youth organizations had brilliant futures before them. At first, however, and despite all my efforts – I'd learned the rules and aims of the Konsomol by heart – I was not allowed to join. Apparently my manners were not "common" enough, and only after a year had passed was I accepted as a "postulant".

Besides the shift in the universities' status, radical changes had been made in university teaching methods. Second-year students were divided up into "brigades" of three or four who were supposed to study together from eight in the morning till two in the afternoon every day. As the people in my brigade knew practically nothing I spent all my mornings teaching them. I can remember taking four hours to explain to one of them a simple formula in physical chemistry – Ostwald's law of electrolytic dissociation. All my efforts were vain, however. My "pupil" asked me several times what "alpha" meant: he had never heard of it before. It suddenly occurred to me to ask whether he had ever learned any algebra. He said he had not. He and his friends had only spent four years in primary school.

At two we had a couple of hours off for lunch. After that, until ten o'clock at night, we had to take part in seminars, the professor asking the students questions as if he were a schoolmaster. After ten it was time for "social work", which, naturally, was both compulsory and unpaid. As well as having to teach others the precepts of Marxism-Leninism, we were also responsible for keeping our own living quarters clean.

Other "social work" took place outside the university. Every year the students had to work for a month or two on state farms (*sovkhozes* or *kolkhozes*). For days on end we harvested potatoes, for which all we were given to eat was a piece of black bread washed down with a glass of milk, though this was a distinct improvement on the horrible fare provided for us in Moscow.

Sunday was a *subotnik* or Communist form of Saturday[28], when we helped in the building of the Metro or in the sorting of fruit and vegetables. Most of the labour involved in constructing the Metro was supplied by students and office workers, who performed the basic tasks of shifting the earth and transporting the stones and bricks. The completed underground stations were magnificent, in stark contrast to the wretched conditions in which the people of Moscow lived.

The appearance of the capital had changed dramatically since the late 1920s. Cobbled streets had been tarred over, and horse-drawn vehicles, like the *teleg*, for merchandise, and the *tarantass*, for passengers, had gradually been superseded by motor cars and vans. As for shops, instead of legends like "Mode de Paris", "Café romain" or "Pâtisserie viennoise" their windows now exhibited stark placards reading "Bread" or "Meat" or "Milk" or

"Fruit and Vegetables". Clothes too had been "proletarianized": the men had exchanged their tweed three-piece suits and trilby hats for caps and lined cotton overalls, while the women had put aside unwieldy hats and constricting corsets for simple khaki dresses and white woollen headscarves.

The centre of the city was in a state of upheaval. The monastery in Pushkin Square had been demolished, together with 80 per cent of the 600 churches Moscow had possessed before the Revolution. The old wall in Lubianka Square had been knocked down to make way for a grandiose Metro station. The noble Sukharevskaya Tower had disappeared, too: it was in the way of the traffic. Here and there tall, aggressively geometrical blocks of flats were gradually rising up. A book on "great socialist achievements" went so far as to boast of the "progress" represented by the destruction of a magnificent baroque cathedral and its replacement by a concrete "agricultural unions centre" in the shape of a combine harvester. Life had become dull and dreary, and for a long while I found myself unable to get over the disappearance of the old Moscow.

Working conditions at the university were also becoming more and more intolerable. Finally, even young and inexperienced as I was, I spoke my mind, telling my fellow students, "The brigade prevents me from working." They rounded on me at once, although one of them did come to my defence. He told me later on that if he had not intervened I might have been thrown out of the university for good.

Any criticism of the establishment was harshly repressed. The mildest punishment was expulsion from the university; the most common was arrest. Meetings involving more than two people were regarded with the greatest suspicion. Informing on others was common, as my friend, the young man who had helped me out after my unfortunate remark about the brigade, learned by bitter experience: he was denounced because his well-kept hands betrayed his "non-proletarian origins". Moreover, students who took an interest in science were guilty of the terrible sin of "academicism".

Eventually even the officials at the Ministry of Education recognized that teaching by means of brigades was completely ineffectual, and after two years of that ill-fated experiment, lectures and examinations were restored. All the students and professors, including the Dean, voted in favour of a return to traditional methods, denouncing the "brigade" approach as vehemently as they had recently defended it.

Meanwhile, the students' living conditions only grew worse. Those who came from peasant or working-class backgrounds were best off, but even with their grants of 30 roubles a month they did not have enough to live decently. Their suits were worn threadbare at knees and elbows, and they had holes in the soles of their shoes. My own shoes were no better, so that, try as I might to reinforce them with newspaper, rainy days meant streaming colds.

In 1931 and 1932 the students in the zoology department, where I was studying, had no more than 200 grams of bread a day. The faculty of mechanical engineering and mathematics was more highly regarded, and the students there had 400 grams. Apart from bread we had practically nothing to eat. The food in the university canteen was dreadful, consisting merely of ersatz replacements politely known as "substitutes". These were croquettes made of mouldy potatoes and rotten meat, although that did not stop a crowd of down-and-outs from falling upon our

74

leavings. After our meal we used to drink tea made from some unknown herbs, stirring it with a spoon that was chained to the samovar. Consuming such stuff all the year round, we suffered permanently from stomach ache.

In my third year I was allowed to go for a holiday to the sanatorium at Gelendjik on the Black Sea. For three days I enjoyed myself bathing, but on the fourth day we were told that our university union had sent more students to the sanatorium than there were places available, so only those who were "socially useful" could stay. I was in despair when I found my name was on the list of students who were "not socially useful", and that I had twenty-four hours to pack. My seaside holiday was over almost before it had begun.

Life was to become even more difficult, however. I can still recall the day when the Dean of our university, a woman, summoned the whole zoology department and told us that all third-year students and those senior to them were to have their grants withdrawn. Only the students from the "useful classes" in the first and second years would go on being subsidized. Everyone fell silent. Then a third-year student called Gololobov declared that he was both a worker and the son of a worker, and now he would no longer have any resources. Despite everything, the assembly reacted with clamorous disapprobation. Everyone, beginning with the Dean, started calling him a "class enemy". He was immediately expelled from the university, and for a long time afterwards Gololobov and "gololobovism" were held in abhorrence.

As I have shown, my life at the university was hardly easy. After much reflection, therefore, I realized that my best hope was to accept my father's – and Vorobiov's – suggestion that I join the team of scientists responsible for the preservation of Lenin's body. As well as providing me with a salary the job would also give me access to the materials and equipment I needed for my own scientific research.

At that time I had no experience of embalming. I did, however, know something of what my father and Vorobiov had been doing, and I started studying the history of mummification in ancient Egypt and elsewhere. It was at once plain that the practice was not a modern one. Various different methods were developed in the Andes, among the Guanches of the Canary Islands, and in Australia, Japan, China and the Phoenician colonies. It was in ancient Egypt, however, that the art reached its highest peak.

Egyptian embalming was always associated with a religious ritual performed by a caste of priests or sacrificers who practised a kind of division of labour. First, a "paraschyte" would make an incision in the dead person's left side. He would then have to run out of the house to avoid being stoned by an angry crowd seeking to punish him for profaning the sacred remains. Next a second type of sacrificer, the "taricheute", came on the scene. It was his job to remove the dead person's entrails, place them in a special receptacle, and throw them from the left bank of the Nile into the water, meanwhile offering up a prayer lauding the piety of the deceased.

These rites aroused a sense of the supernatural in me, while the word "paraschyte" suggested a hint of sacrilege. As I read about those ancient necromancers I imagined myself one of them, and early on during my time in the mausoleum I thought of writing a kind of novel about our team, which I was going to call *The Paraschytes*. Very soon, however, my work on Lenin's body was to prove to be much more humdrum than I had anticipated.

VI

My Early Days at the Mausoleum

"A man sleeping"

I entered the mausoleum for the first time in January 1934 as assistant to Professor Vorobiov and my father. The first thing that struck me was the solemnity of the place. In the middle of a room plunged in semi-darkness stood Lenin's catafalque, an impressive bronze structure with moulded pillars and a cone-shaped lid, inside which narrow beams of pallid light converged, through a flat glass cover, on the dead man's face and hands.

As we took up our positions around the sarcophagus I could hear the hum of an electric mechanism, whereupon pistons situated at the four corners gradually raised the glass lid. We took hold of the body by the legs and shoulders and transferred it to an operating table on castors. A pair of heavy steel doors then opened, and we wheeled the corpse into an adjoining room with white-tiled walls that had been washed down with surgical spirit and antiseptics.

The preservation process involved, first of all, removing Lenin's jacket and trousers, which were kept in place with laces tied behind the back. As I moved the arms I could tell from the touch of the skin, which was yellowish-white in colour, that it had retained its natural elasticity. I found the sensation disagreeable. Since, during my university studies, I had often handled dead bodies without experiencing the slightest discomfort, I was surprised to find it different with the body of Lenin. Not till I was outside the mausoleum again did I realize the reason for my repugnance: it was because Lenin was not an ordinary "stiff", but the venerated – or hated – symbol of an entire nation.

Professor Vorobiov and my father had been visiting the mausoleum twice a week since 1924 to inspect Lenin's face and hands, the only parts of the body visible to the public. The routine they carried out on these occasions consisted merely of smearing the skin with "balsam" to prevent it from drying up and wrinkling. A general overhaul was a different matter, however. This took place about every eighteen months, and while it was going on the mausoleum was completely closed to the public.

Beneath his uniform Lenin was wrapped in rubber bandages, and we would inject "balsam" into the body inside this covering to ensure that the skin as a whole was constantly impregnated with the fluid. Once the bandages were removed, the body was lowered into a large glass bath full of glycerine and potassium acetate. This was the solution known as "balsam", and which had been devised by Professor Vorobiov in 1924.

As we have seen, the first embalming of Lenin, carried out just after his death according to the method most popular at the time, had done little to promote long-term preservation. A. I. Abrikosov had injected into the dead man's aorta 30 measures of formalin, 20 measures of alcohol, 20 of glycerine, 10 of chlorine and 100 of water. This mixture was intended to maintain the body in a state of stability until the funeral five days later.

The somewhat primitive nature of this process, together with the endless arguments between politicians and scientists about the best method to adopt (see Chapter II), resulted in so serious a deterioration of the body that immediate burial had to be seriously considered. The corpse had turned sallow, with more marked discolouration around the eyes, nose, ears and temples. Wrinkles and a purplish stain had appeared over the frontal and parietal lobes of the brain. The skin had sunk in over an area, roughly a centimetre in diameter, at the place where the skull had been opened to extract the brain. The tip of the nose was covered in dark pigments, and the walls of the nostrils had become paper thin; the eyes were half open and sinking into their sockets; the lips had parted, leaving the teeth clearly visible; brown spots had appeared on the hands, and the fingernails were tinged with blue.

All these details were carefully noted by a special committee responsible for establishing the state of the corpse at the end of March, before the second embalming began. It was also on this occasion that my father asked the architect Alexander Pasternak, Boris's brother, to record in watercolour the tones of nine different parts of Lenin's body. This was because Vorobiov wanted to avoid being held solely responsible for the deterioration of the body should his own team's attempt at embalming fail.

Finally, on 26 March 1924, about two months after Lenin's death, Professor Vorobiov and his assistants Arnold Shabadach, Alexander Juravlev and Yakov Zambovski, aided by Professor of Anatomy Piotr Karuzin and my father, were at least able to set to work. The proceedings, which Vorobiov expected to last four months, took place in a cold gloomy cellar underneath the temporary mausoleum.

My father told me later how much he was affected by the sight of the partially decayed corpse, the smell of decomposition emanating from it, and the enormous responsibility resting on the embalmers' shoulders. Now that he, who had moved heaven and earth to get Vorobiov involved in this venture, found himself face to face with the body, he was momentarily at a loss: he had had no experience of working on corpses.

Vorobiov, on the other hand, was in his element. He began by getting rid of the sutures that had been used to sew up the head and chest after the autopsy. Then, having removed the lungs,

July 1924, a month after the embalming was completed. The political and scientific officials responsible for the embalming pose together. Among them can be recognized: seated in front: Benjamin Guerson, Felix Dzerzhinsky's secretary (second from left); Boris Zbarsky (third from left); Abraham Belenky, head of Lenin's guard (fourth from left). Second row: Professor Vorobiov (sixth from left); Felix Dzerzhinsky (seventh from left); R.A. Peterson, commandant of the Kremlin (eighth from left); Avel Yenukidze, secretary of the Central Executive Committee (ninth from left); Kliment Voroshylov, member of the Politburo (far right).

liver, spleen and other viscera, he ordered the inside of the ribcage to be flushed out with distilled water. He next fixed the tissues with formalin,[29] a powerful antiseptic which also inhibits autolysis. Wads of cotton wool steeped in a 1-per-cent solution of formaldehyde were laid over the face, hands and body. After the body cavities had been cleaned out with acetic acid, formalin was injected into such areas of tissue as showed signs of softening. In late March the outside temperature was below zero, and as this was too low for the work of anatomical conservation Vorobiov had stoves installed in the cellar to bring the temperature up to 16 degrees C.

The next step was to immerse the body in a 3-per-cent solution of formaldehyde. Vorobiov, however, did not want to use an ordinary metal bath, the surface of which might interact chemically with components of the liquid. Only a glass bath would rule out such a risk, but frantic appeals from the OGPU to all the laboratories in Moscow succeeded only in proving that no such bath was to be found in Russia. Dzerzhinsky therefore promised to have one made within twenty-four hours, and called in Comrade Kurochkin, who ran a small glassworks. The latter, however, told him that under current conditions it was impossible to produce a glass bath at such short notice.

Vorobiov then considered the possibility of a rubber bath, and Dzerzhinsky went in person to a rubber factory on the outskirts of Moscow. He was disappointed – to say the least – to find that as it was a Saturday no one was working. He therefore scoured the whole neighbourhood until he found the manager, and then made him sound the factory alarm. This brought the workers who lived near by running, thinking there was a fire. They were taken aback to find themselves being ordered to make a rubber bath by the head of the secret police, but the order was at once carried out.

As a result, the following Monday Lenin could at last be put in his rubber bath. Immersed in the viscous liquid, he looked like some strange marine creature. The noxious fumes given off by the formalin (formaldehyde is poisonous) irritated the eyes, noses and chests of the embalmers. As it was, they were hardly able to stand, having now worked for some days practically without sleep. On hearing how exhausted they were, however, Dzerzhinsky sent for my father and said that at the present rate they wouldn't last long enough to finish the job. In reply, my father pointed out that the corpse had to be kept under constant observation during the embalming process. At this Dzerzhinsky promised to arrange for the experts to work in two shifts so that they could get at least a minimum of rest. Three hours after this conversation a contingent of workers and engineers arrived in Red Square. There they installed a tramcar, equipped with beds and electric stoves and all sorts of crockery, for Vorobiov's team to use.[30]

In the meantime, the immersion of the body in the formalin bath had not produced the desired results. The tissues had not absorbed the fluid sufficiently, which meant that incisions would have to be made in the skin and muscles. This prospect worried Vorobiov, however, for he was afraid that he might later be criticized for mutilating the sacred remains of the leader of the world proletariat. He asked Professors V.N. Rozanov and B.S. Weissbrod, who had been charged with supervising the operation as a whole, to give him permission to go ahead. Rozanov's reply was not encouraging: "I'm more worried about the living than about the dead in all this," he said. Vorobiov finally took his courage in both hands and made incisions in the abdomen, shoulders, thighs, and back, and in the palms and the webs between the fingers.

Meanwhile the liquid in the bath had been modified. The content was now 20 per cent alcohol, which has the property of improving the colour of the skin and making it more permeable. After six days the percentage of alcohol was increased to 30 per cent, and 20 per cent of glycerine was added. The body remained immersed in this solution for two weeks, and was then put into a mixture of glycerine and water. The tissues gradually recovered their elasticity.

Next, large jars of potassium acetate were poured into the bath, which by the end of June contained 240 litres of glycerine, 110 kilograms of potassium acetate, 150 litres of water and, as a disinfectant, between 1 and 2 per cent quinine chloride. This was the formula adopted for all subsequent treatments of the body, treatments which, even now, still take place beneath the mausoleum every eighteen months.

Vorobiov was not the first Russian scientist to use this process for preserving tissues. In 1895 Professor Melnikov-Razvedenkov, an anatomical pathologist at Moscow University, had concocted a similar solution containing potassium acetate, glycerine and alcohol. In the course of his researches Melnikov-Razvedenkov had observed that potassium acetate is highly hygroscopic, and that this power to absorb and retain water helps prevent loss of moisture. Similarly, he noted that glycerine preserves the elasticity of tissues and permits the skin to keep its natural colour. It may be said, therefore, that Professor Vorobiov's real distinction lies in his adopting and improving upon Melnikov-Razvedenkov's method.

One of the main difficulties encountered by Lenin's embalmers was the appearance of dark spots on the skin, especially on the deceased's face and hands. In the event Vorobiov managed to solve the problem: in between baths the spots were eliminated by

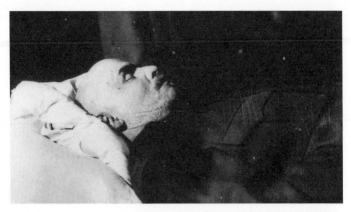

Lenin on his deathbed in Gorky, 22 January 1924, the day after he died.

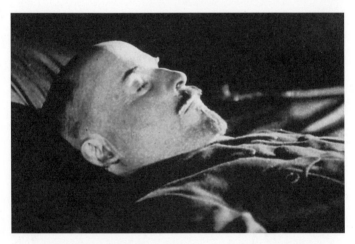

Lenin's body six months later, after completion of the embalming in late July 1924, its condition clearly improved. The skin has regained its original elasticity and colour, while the sewing of the eyelids and the lips prevents any drying-out. As Lenin's brother remarked when he first saw the embalmed body: "He looks as he did when we saw him a few hours after he died – perhaps even better."

the use of a variety of different reagents. For example, if a patch of wrinkling or discolouration occurred it was treated with acetic acid diluted with water. Hydrogen peroxide could be used to restore the tissues' original colouring. Damp spots were removed by means of disinfectants like quinine or carbolic acid.

Once these visible defects had been attended to, there remained the restoration of the eyes and mouth. Stitches were inserted under the dead man's moustache to close the lips. False eyes replaced the real ones to prevent the sockets from becoming too sunken; then the eyelids were closed again and sewn in place.

My father was asked to go and get some of Lenin's clothes from his widow, Nadezhda Krupskaya. She had been opposed to the whole idea of embalming and doubted whether it could be done successfully, but she handed over a khaki-coloured

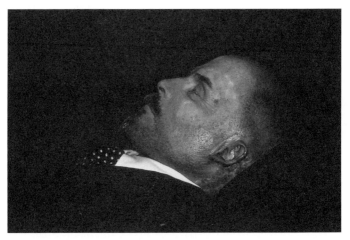

Lenin's body as it really is without being protected by a glass and a soft light (flashlight photograph taken in the mausoleum). Contrary to a persistent legend, the corpse is still preserved in its entirety.

tunic, resembling military uniform, which Lenin had worn at Gorky during his illness.

In the middle of June 1924 Dzerzhinsky gave orders for the body to be dressed and placed in a cone-shaped glass coffin. When all was ready, Nadezhda Krupskaya and Lenin's brother and sisters were invited to come and see the embalmed corpse. Vorobiov and my father awaited their verdict anxiously, but when they heard Dimitri Ulyanov,[31] Lenin's brother, give his opinion they heaved a sigh of relief. "I'm very moved," he said. "It takes my breath away. He looks as he did when we saw him a few hours after he died – perhaps even better."

While, below ground, the work of embalming was finished, on the surface the construction of the new mausoleum was still going on. Larger than the temporary mausoleum, the new structure – also of wood – was completed in July 1924. It was a rectangular building surmounted by a low stepped pyramid of six levels, decreasing in size towards the summit. The face of the second "step" bore the word "LENIN" in large black Cyrillic capitals. A small portico, its roof supported by thirteen square columns, formed the apex of the pyramid. Two flights of steps led up to viewing stands at the front of the building, for the Soviet leaders wanted it to serve not only as a monument to Lenin, but also as a viewing rostrum from which they themselves could watch the military parades designed to glorify Soviet power.

The new edifice upset the general balance of Red Square, however, and so it was decided to modify the latter. A statue commemorating the victory of the Russian forces over the Polish invader in 1920 was moved, and the hulking great plaster figure of a worker, symbol of the October Revolution, was knocked down. In 1929 the second mausoleum was replaced

Summer 1924. The building of the second wooden mausoleum at the centre of Red Square, near the Kremlin ramparts. A rostrum is located on the first terrace.

Inauguration of the second mausoleum, July 1924.

Some of the entries in the international architectural competition held by
the Party for the building of the third mausoleum. None of these was
accepted and in the end the entry by Chtchussev, who had designed
the two previous mausoleums, was chosen.

*The new, permanent, mausoleum under construction where the wooden ones
had stood. Since the general balance of Red Square was altered,
some redevelopment works were ordered.*

by a third, similar in shape but made of red and black granite.

During the ten years that followed the opening of the second mausoleum, Vorobiov and his assistants continually improved the state of the body. In 1934 the few foreigners allowed to visit the mausoleum were unstinting in their praises. "I'm standing beside Lenin," said the American scientist Fertridge. "The man himself. Can it be true he died ten years ago? Wasn't it only yesterday? I really feel I'm looking at a man sleeping. You find yourself walking on tiptoe so as not to wake him. In preserving the body of its historic leader the USSR has achieved the seemingly impossible. The embalming of Lenin is the most perfect example I've ever seen of the art – better even than the mummies of ancient Egypt. Don't the Russian scientists say Vladimir Ilich's body may be preserved for all eternity, without ever suffering the ravages of time?"[32]

Masons finish polishing the granite mausoleum inaugurated in 1930.

VII

The Years of Terror

"The Zbarsky bactericide"

On 1 December 1934, while listening to German radio, I was astounded to hear that Sergei Kirov, First Secretary to the Party in Leningrad, had been found murdered at the Smolny Institute. It was the first time we ever learned publicly of the killing of a leading Party member.

The circumstances surrounding the murder seemed mysterious, to say the least. The murderer, a man called Nikolayev, was summarily executed, and Kirov's bodyguard died in a car accident on the day after the murder. Kirov had been close to Stalin, and many members of the Party regarded him as the latter's potential successor; indeed, he was said to have won a quarter of the votes in the election for the post of General Secretary, although he had not even been a candidate. Had Stalin resented his popularity? Had he deliberately got rid of him? Whatever the answers to these questions, in the months following Kirov's death a wave of terror broke over the country, Leningrad being particularly badly hit, that city seeing large numbers of arrests and deportations. We did not know then that Kirov's murder would mark the beginning of a series of bloody purges inside the Party.

At the mausoleum, too, we were starting to feel the hardening of the political situation. The guard was strengthened and its commanding officer was given a deputy. The experts who dealt with the lighting, heating and refrigeration systems were carefully screened. Nor was it as easy as before to get into the mausoleum, since the guards now had to be informed in advance of each of our visits. We were not allowed to examine the corpse alone; at least two of us had to be present. These precautions only made us more apprehensive. We knew that our every remark, our every gesture, was being carefully noted and reported to the NKVD, the organization which, that year, had succeeded the OGPU and to which the non-scientific staff of the mausoleum belonged.

One of the chief reasons for the stepping-up of security at the mausoleum was an attempted attack that had taken place on 19 March 1934. Mitrofan Nikitin, a peasant employed on a sovkhoze in the Moscow region, entered the mausoleum as a visitor and pulled a revolver out of his pocket. Just as he was about to fire at Lenin's corpse he was overpowered by the guards, but managed to shoot himself in the head.

The NKVD searched Nikitin's house, where they found a letter he had written about atrocities connected with the famine of 1933. "I can't describe all I've seen. I've seen men fall down like flies in the street, in broad daylight. And we've been forced to eat things that even pigs can't stomach . . . " Another passage further on read: "In the spring of 1934, millions of people will die of hunger, filth, and epidemics. There will be a lot of defections from the sovkhozes, the kolkhozes and the factories. Even more than last spring. Our leaders, entrenched inside the walls of the Kremlin, won't see that the people don't want this sort of life – that they have no strength or will left. The younger generation are crippled by hunger and a ridiculous system of education. They are crippled physically and mentally. Everything that's wholesome, good and decent dies every day . . . I, Nikitin Mitrofan Mihailovich, die happily for my country. As I die I protest in the name of millions of workers: enough of slavery, terror, famine and cruelty. Leaders, where are you leading the nation? We are on the slippery slope to the abyss." This letter was passed to Stalin, who added a laconic note: "For my files."[33]

While Lenin, of course, could not die again, other Party leaders could and did, often, like Kirov, in mysterious circumstances. One day in 1937, the caretaker of my building told me when I came home from work that Grigori Ordzhonikidze, a member of the Politburo, had committed suicide. According to the papers and the radio, he had died of an embolism. Yet the forensic surgeon who examined the body told me seven years later, swearing me to secrecy, that there had been a bullet wound in the head. Was Ordzhonikidze killed on Stalin's orders, or did he kill himself? Despite the doubts that persist to this day, the truth will probably never be known.

Fear had finally touched our own family. The NKVD had set seals on thirty-four of the thirty-six flats in the block where my father lived. We nicknamed the place the "DOPR", an acronym of the Russian words meaning both "government house" and "house of provisional imprisonment". All our neighbours were arrested. Most of them died in the labour camps run by the Gulag,[34] among them the Alliluyevs, the family of Stalin's second wife, Nadezhda, who had apparently committed suicide some years earlier. Stalin meant to make them pay dearly for her end.

In November 1932, at a banquet in the Kremlin to mark the fifteenth anniversary of the October Revolution, Nadezhda

Alliluyeva had found the courage to voice her disapproval of her husband's policy of repression against the peasants. Stalin brutally put her down, and she returned to her own quarters, weeping. Next day she was found lying dead in bed, a Walther automatic pistol her brother had given her by her side. It was never known whether she killed herself or if Stalin had had her eliminated. The newspapers, naturally, said she had died of natural causes.

The "government house" where we lived had been built on a marsh beside the Moskva, and looked like a floating block of concrete peppered with tiny windows. It dated from the late 1920s, and some of the most distinguished members of the regime lived there: the veteran Bolshevik, N. Podvoisky; General M.N. Tukhachevsky, hero of the Civil War; M.M. Litvinov, the Foreign Minister from 1933–9; and many members of the Central Committee.

In 1931 my father had been allocated a large five-room flat overlooking a street leading to the Kremlin. It had gas and hot water laid on, a real luxury in those days, and was comfortably if conventionally furnished. I can still see the drawing room with its grand piano, Gothic-style wooden chairs, and armchairs upholstered in Cordovan leather. I also remember a statuette of a gypsy dancing girl brandishing a dagger, and busts of Dante and Beatrice. These had all come from the German industrialist's town house in which we had lived in the 1920s, when it had become the Institute of Biochemistry. In our new place my father took the largest room for his study; I had the smallest.

By the mid-1930s Professor Boris Zbarsky had become an established member of the nomenklatura. Although he had gone slightly grey at the temples, and had acquired a somewhat more

95

solid figure as he approached fifty, he had also gained plenty of self-confidence. Nor was he inclined to criticize his benefactors. When I spoke of the arrests that were taking place all the time in Moscow, his only comment was, "It's no concern of ours." He was a member of the Party, and in 1933 had inherited the chair of biochemistry at the Moscow First Medical Institute. The following year, on the tenth anniversary of the death of the USSR's founding father, he had been awarded the Order of Lenin, an immense honour that also brought with it certain material advantages.

In the spring my father would take us out to our dacha at Serebreniy Bor (Silver Wood), driving us in our Pobeda (Victory), a heavy grey car with glittering steel bumpers. Serebreniy Bor was where the members of the Central Committee went to spend the summer, and on our walks we would catch glimpses, beyond the tall fences surrounding them, of their imposing two-storey wooden villas. Our own dacha had no fewer than seven rooms. The furniture, though, was nothing special: a desk in the Swedish style with lots of drawers, a hammock, and some oak tables and chairs. Dressed in dark blue jackets and straw hats, we could stroll down to the banks of the Moskva in a few minutes. In those days the river there was still clean and clear, with waterlilies floating on it. It was only after the Second World War that factories upstream of the capital started discharging their dirty-yellow waste into the river.

Yet even though I undeniably enjoyed a good deal of material comfort under my father's roof, my stepmother's senseless nagging and bullying finally made me decide to go and live with my mother. I stayed with her until I completed my studies, although her standard of living was very different from what I had become used to with my father. She worked as an assistant

My father, Boris Ilich Zbarsky, during his golden years, in 1936 or 1937.
At that time he held the chair of biochemistry of the Moscow First Medical
Institute, and member of the Moscow Soviet. He is wearing the insignia
of the Order of the Red Flag of Labour and of the Order of Lenin.

in a hospital lab, analysing medical tests in return for a salary barely enough to keep one person. She lived in an old building in the Arbat district, sharing a flat with six other families – twenty-three people in all. You had to queue for practically everything: meals, bathroom, lavatory, telephone. There were wires stretched across the room to dry the washing. A piece of paper on the front door read, "Ring once for the Zbarskys. Ring twice for the Marks," and so on. There was virtually no privacy, and what little there might have been was compromised by some of the neighbours, who listened at doors and thus knew every detail of my mother's sex life.

Occasionally she would entertain one of her lovers in her bedroom, a large, light room which still bore a few traces of earlier days. The ceiling was covered with trompe-l'œil rural scenes of sheep grazing and satyrs playing the flute. The furniture was sparse enough: an oblong table of Karelian birch; a brown sofa with an oriental rug thrown over it; three low threadbare armchairs; a large oval mirror in front of which my mother used to preen in fine lace dresses and hats with veils that she had worn before the First War. It was not much of a love nest. The pale brown wallpaper was covered with patches of damp; none of the latches worked on the doors and windows; big brown drops leaked from the water main. The flat, which had probably once belonged to some rich merchant family, had not had any repairs done to it since the Revolution.

My mother, however, never complained about her new existence, for she knew that she shared the same lot as 95 per cent of the Muscovites. The population of the city had greatly expanded as a result of the October Revolution. People from the provinces, hoping for great things from the new regime, had flocked to the capital, while domestic servants, who before had lived in the basements, were rehoused on the other floors. The Soviet authorities, imposing the sharing of accommodation as a matter of principle, hoped thereby to wean people away from the instinct to own private property.

By an ironical twist of fate, one of my mother's flatmates was Maxime Mark, son of the German industrialist who had precipitately left Russia after the Revolution, and some of whose furniture, requisitioned for the Institute of Biochemistry, was now being used by my father. Maxime, however, although he knew about this, never made any attempt to reclaim his family's property. He was a convinced Communist, opposed to the whole principle of inheritance. His mother, an enormously wealthy bourgeoise living in Sweden, begged him to go and join her, but he steadfastly refused. He believed that his destiny lay in the homeland of socialism, a choice he was to live to regret bitterly.

One night in 1937 the manager of the building came to our flat with three men from the NKVD, asking to see Maxime Mark. "Citizen," said one of the policemen, "you're under arrest. You've got half an hour to pack your things." At this, all the doors in the apartment flew open and parents, grandparents and children crowded out into the ill-lit corridor. Then, seeing the sinister expressions of the burly leather-clad NKVD men, they all fell silent. We heard a woman sobbing. It was Alexandra Konstantinovna, Mark's wife. "Don't worry," he told her. "Everything will be all right – you'll see." He kissed his family goodbye and vanished down the corridor carrying a small case. We never saw him again; we learned later that he had died in a camp in the Far East.

In those days death might knock at your door at any moment.

Fear of the Soviet state was such that it undermined confidence and trust even within families. This syndrome did not spare our family, either.

In 1935 the Soviet intelligence services, the NKVD, contacted my father and gave him a booklet containing the secret formula for a powerful bactericide. The document had been stolen by one of their agents from an American laboratory. The product was still unknown in the USSR, and my father was given the job of converting the formula into fact. Since he did not speak English himself, he asked me to translate the document. "But it's absolutely essential we don't say where it came from," he said. "Once the stuff is made I shall officially be the one who discovered it. Those are government orders."

Armed with the translation, he instructed his colleagues at the institute and me to carry out the necessary chemical procedures. These resulted in an organic compound of mercury, of which phenylmercuronitrate was the main ingredient. The process involved our having to melt mercury acetate at high temperature, working under a hood fitted with an air pump. The scientists who assisted my father were paid nearly double their usual salaries and replaced every month. It was different for me, however. He made me work for several months for nothing, declaring that it was not proper to claim money from the state in his own name.

After toiling for two and a half months under the hood I was suffering from terrible headaches, hair loss and bleeding gums. Alarmed by these symptoms, I tried to find out what had caused them. I discovered that mercury fumes, and above all those given off in the synthesizing process, were toxic, and that inhaling them could lead ultimately to illness or even death. I told my father about my aches and pains, and asked him to let me quit the team without more ado. He would not hear of it; instead, he told me my sufferings were imaginary and ordered me to go on as before. I was in despair.

Not knowing what to do, I waited for Professor Vorobiov's next visit and told him my woes. He was taken aback, and rushed furiously into my father's study. I could hear him shouting from the next room. "Have you gone mad? You're killing your own son!" Since Vorobiov was senior to my father in the hierarchy, he got his way and the next day I was let off. I went to see Vorobiov in his office, threw my arms round him and vowed eternal gratitude.

Even now I still find it hard to understand my father's attitude. Did he perhaps underestimate the risks? Or, urged on by his previous successes in the service of the regime, was he prepared to sacrifice his son for the sake of his own glory? His callousness in the affair reminded me of someone he fervently admired: Peter

Professor Vorobiov and me.

the Great, who did not hesitate to have his son Alexis murdered for reasons of state.

The drug was finally tested in several hospitals with excellent results, and distributed all over the USSR under the name of the "Zbarsky bactericide". As for me, I was still a constant prey to headaches, and went on feeling the effects of the mercury fumes for several years. My anger against my father reached its height when I found out, years later, that during one of his trips abroad he had undergone a course of anti-mercury treatment. Yet the fumes that reached him in his study in the mausoleum must have been negligible compared to those his colleagues and I had inhaled under the hood. Nor was this the only time my father treated me harshly.

Because my duties in the mausoleum took up only about two-fifths of my working day, I was able to spend the rest of my time on my studies. I had a degree in physiology and had specialized in biochemistry, and I was eager to get a master's degree (in the USSR, the stage before a doctoral thesis). To my astonishment my father opposed this idea. "A thesis!" he cried. "What do you want with a thesis? If you ask me, you've already got everything you need!" Admittedly my work with Lenin's corpse brought me in 200 roubles a month, although that was a fairly modest sum in those days. It also provided me with good facilities for research. The mausoleum had equipment – microscopes, centrifuges, and so on – and supplies of chemicals that were the envy of other research centres in the USSR. All that, however, meant little to me if I could not continue my studies as I wished. My father's reaction plunged me into despair once more. For a moment I thought of working on my thesis at a different laboratory, but after weighing up the pros and cons I concluded it would be too risky. In those days of absolute dictatorship there was no room for individual liberty. My father's position in the Soviet scientific community was so well established that he could influence other directors of studies. I was completely dependent on him. I can only explain his attitude by supposing that he did not want me to progress too far too fast. Perhaps he was afraid my reputation might eclipse his own.

It was not until two years later that, by dint of much insistence, I managed to persuade him to let me prepare my thesis. He agreed only on one condition, however: that he should choose the subject. I was to carry out research into the influence of amino acids on the growth of tumours, which involved carrying out a series of tests on white mice. The results, which were in fact designed to advance my father's career, were mixed; nor did the work really interest me. I did not share my father's ideas on biochemistry. Even then I was mainly concerned with the chemistry of tissues and of cells in general, with cellular nuclei, and with nucleic acids in particular. As I have said, these subjects had been suggested to me by Professor Vorobiov.

Meanwhile the terror continued on its inexorable way. On 6 November 1937, when preparations were being made in Red Square for the ceremony on the following day commemorating the twentieth anniversary of the Revolution, we learned that nearly all the guards at the Kremlin and at the mausoleum had been arrested. Among them was Peterson, the officer in charge of the Kremlin, and Trenin, the officer in charge of the mausoleum. When they were arrested some important documents also disappeared, and it became impossible from then on for us to consult the records containing accounts of our work.

Even as hundreds of thousands of people all over the country were disappearing, the newspapers were lauding the successes of

The Politburo takes the salute at a military parade from the rostrum of the mausoleum in Red Square. From left to right: Molotov, Stalin, Voroshilov, Kalinin, Andreyev, Zhdanov, Chubar (his face erased on the negative because he had already been arrested), and Dimitrov. Two of those present, Stalin and Dimitrov, would later be embalmed by the staff of the building upon which they are standing; Stalin's embalmed corpse would be placed there beside Lenin's from 1953 to 1961.

the socialist economy. In them you could read, for example, that the industrial production of the USSR in one day was equal to that of Tsarist Russia in one year (this was, of course, wholly untrue). And despite our meagre standard of living, it was dinned into us all the year round that the country's economic situation was excellent. You had only to look at the West to be convinced, we were told. France, England and America were beset by terrible poverty, and the workers there were going hungry. Caricatures showed bloated capitalists riding on the backs of their scrawny employees.

In Moscow, meanwhile, rumours were circulating about the arrest of a number of prominent people. When I told my father

I had heard that A.N. Tupolev, the aircraft designer, had been detained, he said it was quite impossible. His reaction was under-standable: Tupolev had designed many of the USSR's combat aircraft, and it seemed to most people that the country was depen-dent on him for much of its military might. Even so, the news of his arrest was later confirmed to us by one of his relations.[35]

In the autumn of 1937 fate dealt the mausoleum staff another blow when Professor Vorobiov experienced a sudden pain in his back which was diagnosed as being due to a malignant tumour. The doctors insisted, quite unnecessarily, that he must have an operation. Vorobiov, however, who was both suspicious and impulsive by nature, refused to be operated on in the Kremlin Hospital. Probably, he remembered the tragic end of Mikhail Frunze who, in 1925, when People's Commissar for Defence, was diagnosed as having a stomach ulcer. Although surgery was unnecessary, Stalin ordered him to undergo an immediate operation. Frunze died on the operating table.

Vorobiov wanted to be treated by his friend Professor A. Melnikov, a surgeon in Kharkov. Unusually for those days, his request was granted, and the operation took place without incident. A few days later, however, Vorobiov's condition suddenly worsened, and on 31 October he died. My father and I immedi-ately went to Kharkov for the funeral of our friend.

The circumstances of Vorobiov's illness and death aroused serious suspicions in me. There was no proof that an operation had been necessary. In any case, it had shown the tumour to be benign. This had not stopped the surgeons from removing his left kidney, however, and the right, weakened, could no longer function adequately. The inevitable happened and Vorobiov died of uraemia. I am still inclined, even today, to attribute his death to a gross error on the part of the doctors. Yet the mistake was so enormous that I cannot help relating the loss of our friend to certain medical practices characteristic of those days. Thousands of doctors, under pressure from the NKVD, saw to it that some "awkward" comrades died in the operating theatre.

Vorobiov had probably been denounced by a member of our own team. He was in the habit, when he'd had too much to drink, of airing his opinions aloud to his friends and colleagues, and occasionally he would say something really indiscreet. I remember him coming back tipsy one night in 1935 from a dinner Stalin had given at the Kremlin to mark the founding of a big medical centre, a kind of prototype of the future Academy of Medical Sciences. Vorobiov went to bed without bothering to undress, and as I was helping him he said triumphantly, "Do you know what? I kissed Stalin." When he was sober he spoke of his dislike for the "dim Georgian".

After Vorobiov died my father became head of the team responsible for preserving Lenin's body. Through another twist of fate, however, he too was struck down by a mysterious illness. The doctors diagnosed a tumour on the left kidney, and decided on an emergency operation in the Kremlin Hospital. The left kidney was duly removed, but soon complications developed and the abdominal cavity became seriously infected, and for a time his life was in danger. As it happened, he recovered after a few weeks, and he was soon able to resume his normal activities.

While he was ill I had a phone call from the NKVD. Its director, Comrade Yezhov, wanted to see me as a matter of urgency. I took my colleague R. Sinelnikov with me to the headquarters of the state police, where we were thoroughly searched before being allowed into the office of the People's Commissar for the Interior, for Yezhov was always afraid of attempts on his life. Not without reason, for during the terrible years from 1936 to 1938 he was head of the organization that sent millions of innocent Soviet citizens to their deaths.[36] We found him sitting in a large office at an imposing desk – a weedy-looking little man with searching eyes. Behind him, to demonstrate his unbounded devotion to the General Secretary, he had hung a huge portrait of Stalin, and a bust and a smaller portrait of the dictator stood on the table.

Having asked us to sit down, Yezhov then rose to his feet and looked us up and down from the height of his five-foot-nothing, looking even more dwarfish than I had imagined him. The Politburo, he declared gravely, had requested him to find out whether the serious state of Professor Zbarsky's health might not have repercussions for the work of preserving Lenin's body. Replying, I began by stressing how greatly we valued Professor Zbarsky's knowledge and experience. But, I went on, even should he die, we were ready to continue with the work of preservation. I had scarcely finished before Sinelnikov jumped up and declared: "Comrade Yezhov, I assure you that the task of preserving Lenin's body is in safe hands, and that we take full responsibility for it."

A few years later, when we were in Tiumen, a small town in Siberia to which Lenin's body had been evacuated after the beginning of the German offensive in 1941, my father asked us how we had answered Comrade Yezhov's questions. Without batting an eyelid, Sinelnikov replied, "Boris Ilich, we said that without you we were completely incapable of going on with the work." This bare-faced and unforgivable lie took my breath away. When I told my father what had really happened he realized at once how untrustworthy Sinelnikov was. As soon as the latter committed some minor offence my father seized the opportunity to get rid of him.

In March 1938 my father and I were given passes to the famous trial of the "rightist Trotskyite bloc," which took place at the House of Trade Unions where, fourteen years earlier, Lenin's body had lain in state. At one end of a long room with off-white walls, once used as a ballroom by the Union of the Nobility, the public prosecutor, the sinister Andrei Vyshinsky (later Foreign Minister from 1949 to 1953), delivered a long and venomous indictment. The main charge was that a "rightist Trotskyite bloc" made up of Party leaders and doctors had attempted to overthrow the Soviet government. Naturally they were spies in the pay of foreign powers; naturally, too, they had tried several times to assassinate Stalin.

The indictment lasted a good two hours, and every accusation appeared to be so strongly backed by evidence that it seemed it must be true. And the depositions of the accused only seemed to confirm their guilt. In the great majority of cases they repented of their crimes and asked Comrade Stalin for forgiveness. The admissions of three of the doctors – Levine, Pletnev and Kazakov – were especially convincing. They confessed that on the orders of People's Commissar for the Interior Yagoda – also one of those accused – they had treated the writer Maxim Gorky, and his son Maxim Pechkov, in such a way as to accelerate their deaths. They had done the same in the cases of such eminent members of the Party as Kuybyshev and Menzhinsky, as also in those of many other less well-known figures. Their testimony went into detail about how they had administered poison to their patients.

These statements made such an impression on me that I became convinced the accused men were guilty. Most of them begged that their lives be spared. Some, like Yagoda, who had been head of the political police between 1934 and 1936, went down on their knees and tearfully implored "beloved Comrade Stalin" to pardon them. It was rumoured later that Stalin had been present at the trial, peering through a spy-hole in the wall and thoroughly enjoying the spectacle.

Rykov and Bukharin were the only two of the accused who bore themselves with dignity. They looked very different from the last time I had seen them, at Rykov's dacha in 1930, for they were now thin and drawn, having probably been subjected to strong-arm interrogation during their time in prison. I felt sorry for them, and distressed at their plight.

Rykov did not plead for mercy. All he said was that his stance within the Party had met with bitter defeat – he had been denounced for "right deviationism" in 1929 for opposing the collectivization of farms and the treatment meted out to the kulaks – and that "any opposition to the General Secretary's own line was pointless and doomed to failure." The man who showed most courage in that terrible ordeal, however, was undoubtedly Bukharin. With superhuman patience he managed to speak for two whole hours, despite the insults hurled at him by NKVD agents in plain clothes placed strategically among the seething audience. "Swine!", "Liar!", "You bring dishonour on Soviet justice!" they kept yelling.

Bukharin began his deposition by denying the existence of any "rightist Trotskyite bloc". "What possible link could there be between Chernov, the Minister of Agriculture, Dr Levine, Dr Kazakov and myself?" he asked, and went on to quote, ironically, a German proverb, "Mit gefangen, mit gehangen" ("Caught together, hanged together"). He even had the audacity to say that the Bolshevik Bukharin did not need any lessons from the former Menshevik Vyshinsky. His analysis of the various phases of Party history showed the senselessness of Vyshinsky's indictment. After only a few minutes his moral and intellectual superiority over his accuser was plain.

His efforts were in vain, however, for it goes without saying that the trial was completely rigged. Rykov and Bukharin, like Yagoda and many others of those accused, were all executed. One could go on for ever discussing the course the trial took and its mixture of truth and lies, but in the end all that is certain is that the accounts of it made public at the time were entirely at odds with the facts. Furthermore, I can speak of it all the more confidently since I am one of the last surviving members of the audience in the courtroom.

Whatever the course of the purges with their show trials, the mausoleum seemed to bask in official favour. On 7 September 1938 my father wrote to Molotov, by now the Chairman of Sovnarkom, suggesting that a small laboratory be attached to the mausoleum for the purpose of improving the techniques used to preserve Lenin's body. He further proposed that the staff of the laboratory should work under the authority of a Party official, and for this task he put forward the name of Commissar for the Interior Yezhov, the chief of the political police (although he too was to fall from favour, being replaced the following year by Laurenti Beria). It would be easier to gain good working conditions with such a protector.

A few months later, on 20 January 1939, just before the fifteenth anniversary of Lenin's death, a special committee of scientists, headed by People's Commissar for Health Nikolai Grashchenkov, was set up to study the condition of the corpse. After a close examination it was pronounced satisfactory. Admittedly there were minor defects here and there: the right eye was half-open, and there were dark spots on the left forearm and the feet. These, however, were dealt with in the presence of the committee. As an added benefaction, the officer in charge of the Kremlin, Nikolai Spiridinov, used this occasion to announce that the government had accepted Professor Zbarsky's suggestion. Orders were therefore given to build the new laboratory, and also to construct a model for a new sarcophagus.

The laboratory was installed in an old building belonging to Moscow University. As well as the team directly responsible for the preservation of the body, the staff now included an excessive and growing number of bureaucrats: technical assistants, administrative personnel and accountants.

During this period, I had continued my studies for my master's degree, in between the times I spent at the mausoleum. In 1938, at the end of my final year at the university, I was appointed to the chair of biological and analytical chemistry at the Medical Institute, and I started teaching biochemistry there. What struck me most at first was how much the educational level of the students had improved since I myself had entered the university in 1931. Among them there was one of about my own age with whom I especially enjoyed talking. One day I asked him why he had come to the university so late. He told me that he had spent seven years in prison for reading Esenin's poetry with his friends at high school. The regime regarded Esenin as not sufficiently "Soviet".

By now, the situation of science in the country as a whole was critical, for those involved in scientific research were short of equipment and very poorly paid. By contrast, our position at the laboratory was very much better, for we were more than well supplied with materials. Moreover, I was able to pursue my researches into subjects that had nothing to do with the preservation of Lenin's corpse. Indeed, working at both the laboratory and the Medical Institute made it easier for me to pursue my studies in the fundamental sciences.

In August 1939 the papers announced the signing of the Nazi-Soviet Pact, usually known as the "Molotov-Ribbentrop Pact", after the Soviet and German Foreign Ministers who had signed it.[37] It hit us like a thunderclap out of a clear blue sky. Only the day before, the Soviet media were fiercely denouncing fascist Germany and the Anti-Comintern Pact of 1936 between Germany and Japan, which pledged their hostility to international communism (Italy joined the pact a year later). After this complete volte-face the papers concentrated their fire on "decaying Anglo-French capitalism". I myself regarded the Molotov-Ribbentrop agreement as tantamount to the USSR's joining the Anti-Comintern Pact; indeed, it was already clear to me that there was no essential difference between fascism and communism.

A few months later I got married, having met my wife, Irina, at Moscow University in 1934, when she was studying genetics there. Two years younger than I, she had fair hair and blue eyes, although what attracted me most was her lively intelligence. She was one of the four daughters of Piotr Karuzin, the famous professor of anatomy, and winning her was no easy matter, although we were finally married in November 1939. After graduating from the university, Irina began working in the histology department of the Moscow First Medical Institute.

One day in 1935 – soon after the "Zbarsky bactericide" episode – I told Irina about my affection and admiration for Professor Vorobiov. She seemed not to know whom I was talking about. I was surprised, as Vorobiov was very well known in anatomical circles; besides, Irina must have been aware that her father had worked with Vorobiov on the embalming of Lenin's corpse in 1924. Nevertheless, for several years after that conversation, Irina's attitude towards me was very guarded. I did not dare ask her the reasons for this sudden coldness, for the times we were living in discouraged the expression of personal feelings. It was only after our marriage in 1939 that she felt she could trust me enough to explain her strange behaviour.

While the work of embalming Lenin's body was making good progress, she told me, her father had invited Vorobiov to dinner. That evening the two eminent professors drank one another's health in alcohol of 96 degrees of proof – duly diluted with water – which had come from the basement stores in the mausoleum and was meant to be used for the embalming of Lenin's corpse. Vorobiov, having grown rather tipsy on this brew, said he wasn't feeling very well, and left the room. After a while Karuzin, wondering where his guest had got to, went all over the house in search of him. Opening a door on the second floor, he found Vorobiov kissing his daughter Lela, one hand on her breast. Beside himself with fury, Karuzin threw Vorobiov out.

The latter swiftly retaliated. On the following day he dismissed Karuzin from the embalming team, on the grounds that he had been misappropriating alcohol from the mausoleum. Nor did Vorobiov's enmity abate with time. In 1930 he campaigned against Professor Karuzin's re-election to the chair of anatomy at the First Medical Institute – and he got his way. Karuzin's academic career came to an abrupt halt.

I was dismayed by what my wife told me. Even though it could not change my feelings for Vorobiov (who by then had been dead for some time, in any case), her story did show him in a new and disturbing light. How could one excuse his deliberate persecution of an elderly professor, whose only crime was to have defended his daughter's honour in his own house? I did in fact know a little about Vorobiov's attitude, for once, in 1935, finding myself alone with the Professor, I had asked him why he had dismissed Karuzin from the team of embalmers. Because, he said, Karuzin had drunk alcohol belonging to the mausoleum. "But you all did that in those days," I objected. "That's got nothing to do with it," he replied. "He did it without my permission."

When I told him that I hoped to marry Irina Karuzin, Vorobiov had frowned. "Be careful," he said. "They're a family of anti-Semites." I was astonished. The Karuzins had never said a word to justify such an accusation; indeed, Irina's father went out of his way to make sure his children should not be prejudiced. She herself remembered how, when she was a child during the famine of the early 1920s, some Jews came to their house offering eggs and vegetables for sale. The cleaning woman referred to them as "Yids", and Irina repeated the word to her father. He became very angry. "Don't ever let me hear you use such expressions!" he exclaimed. Vorobiov was utterly wrong, for if ever there was a family that was not anti-Semitic, it was the Karuzins.

Whatever Professor Vorobiov's faults, his work endured triumphantly. In 1940 an article by Professor Abrikosov appeared in *Izvestiya*, entitled "Sixteen Years of Preserving Lenin's Corpse" and disclosing that between 1924 and 1940 the mausoleum had been visited by more than 16 million people. "This experiment, unique in all the world," wrote Abrikosov, "has made it possible to preserve a man's corpse after his death in a state like that of a living body. It has been conducted by a team of scientists who have enthusiastically carried out the instructions of Comrade Stalin. We rejoice that this great scientific success should be linked to the name of the greatest man in the history of the world: Lenin." Two years earlier, Lenin's widow, Nadezhda Krupskaya, had visited the mausoleum, accompanied by my father. She had praised the work of our team, going so far as to remark that, while she herself was ageing visibly, Lenin and his mausoleum were endowed with eternal youth.

It was amid such wild enthusiasm that we were to find ourselves heading for the second worldwide conflict, later called, in Russia, the "Great Patriotic War". Little did we suspect that in just a few months' time our lives would be turned upside-down.

VIII

The War Years

Taking Lenin's body to Siberia

On Sunday, 22 June 1941, on the stroke of seven in the morning, I was woken up by the telephone. "Have you heard what's on the radio?" asked Sergei Mardashev, one of my colleagues at the mausoleum laboratory. I rushed to my set, only to hear the usual rigmarole about the successes of the socialist economy. Back I hurried to the telephone. "I can't hear anything special," I said. "You must be on the wrong wavelength," replied Mardashev. I switched to a German station and caught a news bulletin. A voice – it proved to be Hitler's – was proclaiming that the USSR was just a "conglomeration of ill-assorted races and nations threatening European civilization". There were references to the claims Molotov had made, during the Berlin negotiations for the Nazi-Soviet Pact, for Russia to have control of the Bosporus, part of Poland, Bessarabia, the Baltic States and Finland, once they had been seized or conquered. "German troops," the Führer concluded, "crossed the Soviet frontier at four o'clock this morning and are advancing rapidly into enemy territory. May God be with them!"

Many years later it was said that Stalin could not believe his ears when he was told about the German invasion. He was so shocked that he shut himself up in his study and refused to see any of his colleagues for several days. Leaders of the Party and of the government didn't know what to do. When they decided they must go in and see him, Stalin made to run away: he thought they had come to arrest him.

Historians tend to be surprised that he should have reacted thus, for there had been plenty of warning signs before the attack: the reports of military and other intelligence bodies, dispatches noting German troop concentrations on the Soviet frontier, the number of enemy aircraft intruding on Russian airspace. British radio daily broadcast lists of the German divisions massed on the Soviet border, and even announced the precise date of Operation Barbarossa. Only Hitler's hysterical monologues and Goebbels's sugary speeches insisted on Germany's indestructible friendship with the USSR, and contrasted the great advantages of socialism with the decadence of the Western democracies. On the radio Hitler maintained that industrial production was in free fall in the rotten capitalist democracies, while in the USSR, the home-land of socialism, it had risen by 40 per cent in the last five years; over the same period Germany herself had increased production by 120 per cent. The Soviet radio repeated these statements and spoke proudly of the strength of Soviet-German friendship, and admiringly of the Nazi invasions of Belgium, France, Holland, Denmark and Norway. For my part, I never believed in all those protestations of friendship. To me, as to many of my contemporaries, the threat of German invasion was clear. Not to Stalin, however. Trusting blindly in Hitler, he ignored the warnings of the people around him, refusing to listen to his generals' urgings that the USSR should prepare to defend itself.

And so on 22 June 1941 the German Army, taking advantage of the fact that many of our soldiers and frontier guards were on leave, easily broke through our lines of defence and, after destroying hundreds of Soviet aircraft on the ground, struck deep into our territory.

Meanwhile, in Moscow, everything seemed perfectly calm. There was no sign of panic. The radio went on broadcasting the same cheerful music and the same reports on the achievements of the national economy. At twenty minutes before noon, however, it was announced on the radio that Comrade Molotov, the Chairman of Sovnarkom and also Foreign Minister, was going to broadcast to the nation. In a faltering voice he told us of the attack by the German Army and the need to organize our defence. The enemy's troops were advancing swiftly towards Moscow. The danger that the capital might be shelled or bombed grew greater every day.

Faced with this alarming situation, one of the first things the Politburo decided, on 26 June 1941, was to transfer Lenin's body to Tiumen, a small town in western Siberia. On the same day Poskrebychev, Stalin's secretary, informed the secretary of the local Party in Tiumen that an "object" of exceptional importance would soon be arriving in his town. This information was to be kept strictly confidential. The choice of Tiumen was no accident: since it lay beyond the Urals and well away from the big industrial centres, it was unlikely to be the target of air raids.

Of the senior staff who made up the inner circle at the mausoleum, only my father was told of this decision. He was personally made responsible for preparing a coffin suitable for transporting the body, and for selecting the necessary equipment to go with it. The existing coffin was therefore placed in a large wooden crate, and the consignment also included two glass baths and the chemicals and equipment necessary for preserving Lenin's body.

Professor Mardashev and I were not told of its destination until 3 July. That evening we were picked up with our families at our homes by NKVD cars and driven to a siding at Yaroslavl station, where a closely guarded special train was waiting for us. I remember that on the way to the station we listened to a speech by Stalin, the first he had made since the outbreak of hostilities. "Comrades, brothers and sisters, my friends, I speak to you in a solemn hour", he began, going on to praise the achievements and victories of the Russian people. It was the first time he had addressed the nation so warmly. I had never heard his voice before, and have to admit to being surprised by his strong Georgian accent and faulty pronunciation. In what is still a famous speech he called on the population to burn and destroy any territory occupied by the enemy so as to make it impossible for the Germans to live off the land in those areas of our country they had occupied.

By now the mausoleum we were leaving looked quite different. It was covered in metal scaffolding over which was spread a black tarpaulin. This cumbersome camouflage was removed on 7 November 1941, at the time of the historic parade of the defenders of Moscow, whose heroism and sacrifice had turned back the Germans almost on the city's outskirts.

The train left at nine in the evening of a very hot July day. The plane-wood coffin containing Lenin's body had been coated with paraffin, and its lid moved along grooves greased with vaseline. The windows of the special carriage were curtained, and we took it in turns to watch over the body day and night.

Kiryushin, the officer responsible for guarding the mausoleum, was also on the train, with his family and a detachment of officers and men from the Kremlin. In all, some forty people were there to look after "post number one". Red Army sentries were stationed at intervals along the roads that ran alongside the tracks, to protect the train from attack. At the stations we passed through, soldiers held off people trying to flee to the east to escape German air raids.

We reached Tiumen on 7 July, to be welcomed by the town authorities: Secretary of the Party Committee D.S. Kuptsov, Chairman of the Council, S.I. Zagrignayev, and departmental head of the NKVD S.I. Kozov. It was not until we arrived that they found out what the "secret object" was that Stalin's secretary had told them to prepare for. The next day the "object" was transferred to a squat two-storey building belonging to the local

The 'Tiumen mausoleum' in western Siberia, the building where Lenin's corpse was kept during the Second World War, previously a school of agriculture. The "funeral chamber" was on the first floor.

school of agriculture. The place was surrounded by a brick wall surmounted by a spiked rail, and stood completely apart from the rest of the town. It was very dirty inside, and the plumbing left a lot to be desired, so that we had to have it almost completely overhauled. After we moved in the place was renamed "NKVD House", though the inhabitants called it the "White House" because of its colour.

The body was put on the first floor in one of the wings of the house. The windows of the room it was in were walled up to protect the coffin from sunlight, and the plaster was all made good and the walls repainted. Our laboratory was installed in the adjoining rooms. At the end of July another special train arrived with all the equipment we needed for our research, including supplies of chemicals and refrigerating apparatus. It was all put in an "equipment room", next to the "funeral chamber". Thus a whole new temporary mausoleum was gradually assembled on the first floor of the building in Tiumen.

At first we encountered certain practical difficulties. For instance, we could only get the distilled water we needed for the bath in which Lenin's body was periodically soaked from Omsk, several hundred kilometres away. Such problems aside, however, our working conditions were reasonably satisfactory. We had no fixed hours, and spent most of our time making minor repairs to the corpse. The building we worked in was cleaned from top to bottom, the floor covered with linoleum, the walls painted and the ceiling replastered. As for our main work, the body was regularly immersed in a bath of "balsam", and we set about systematically eliminating the remaining defects noted by the 1939 inspection committee. In Tiumen we had more time to spend on the body than we'd had in Moscow, so that by the time our stay there ended in 1945 the condition of the corpse had improved considerably. It had, in effect, undergone a kind of re-embalming.

During the terrible war years the people of Tiumen endured hardships of many kinds: rationing left them close to starvation, and there were shortages of electricity, heating, water and so on. Thanks to the town authorities, however, we enjoyed privileged living conditions. Our building was always well lit, and we had plenty to eat. In a sense our lifestyle was ideal, especially for such hard times. Yet I was troubled by our not being able to fight for our country, as I was by seeing the wounded who came our way being looked after in such inadequate conditions.

The officers and men of the Kremlin guard nevertheless managed to find cause for complaint about the food, something the rest of us thought very odd. In 1942, however, when I had to go to the Kremlin, I understood why they complained. I had never seen such a well-stocked canteen in all my life. While the people of Moscow went hungry, we could order fine dishes, and afterwards take home rarities like butter, cheese, ham and marvellous white bread. Moreover, troops serving in the NKVD in general, and in the Kremlin in particular, enjoyed a number of privileges, of which not the least was that since they were regarded as being "mobilized" already, they did not have to join in the actual fighting. I discovered later that more than two million members of the security services were never obliged to fight. Even in wartime, Stalin, fearing a popular uprising, maintained this large army of informers, secret police, spies, guards, as well as the vast bureaucracy that administered it, to defend both his person and his regime.

Over and above my work on Lenin's body I taught mineral, organic and biological chemistry at the Tiumen teacher training institute; my wife Irina taught biology there as well. Later I also lectured on fundamental chemistry at the Kuban Medical Institute, whose teaching staff and students had been evacuated to Tiumen. Teaching brought me into contact with the inhabitants of the town, and despite the highly confidential reason for our presence the locals eventually came to know what the famous "object" was. Besides, a quick look at any reference work that listed prominent scientists would confirm to anyone the kind of work my father was involved in.

Even though we were 1,500 kilometres from Moscow we took a close interest in the international news, the situation at the front, and in the living conditions of the Muscovites. Most of our information came from foreign radio stations, though we found out what was happening at the front from talking to refugees from the west.

On 16 October 1941 we were appalled to learn that German troops had reached the outskirts of Moscow, and that the capital might fall. The situation became so critical that all the leaders were evacuated. It was announced that a speech by Pronin, Chairman of the Moscow City Council, was to be broadcast. This, though awaited with great concern, turned out to be very insipid for, far from describing the heroic defence of the city, Pronin dwelt on the fact that all the municipal services, public baths, hairdressing salons, and so on were functioning normally. I learned later that after this speech the people of Moscow panicked. Most tried to flee, mobbing trains which, of course, were quite unable to carry them all.

When we went to Moscow in 1942 the officer in charge of our special train, a colonel in the NKVD, took us by way of the Minsk area, 30 kilometres from the capital. On either side of the track there was nothing to be seen but burned-out aircraft, smashed tanks and trucks reduced to heaps of scrap. It was an unforgettable sight, and made us realize how fierce the recent fighting had been.

Meanwhile the people of Moscow were suffering great privations. For most of them, food shortages had proved more of a problem than German bombers. They took heart again when they heard that the Red Army had managed to drive the Germans out of the western suburbs. The enemy were never to come so close to conquering the capital again, and the situation on the front started to improve at the end of 1943. By then, Soviet troops, having driven back the invader in many places, were already fighting on enemy territory. One result of this was that I was then able to go and visit my mother, who had been evacuated to Omsk in western Siberia.

As I have said, we enjoyed a very pleasant lifestyle in Tiumen. As the end of the war approached we had more and more spare time, a good deal of which we spent hunting and fishing. There was plenty of game: duck and grouse in the autumn, hares in the winter. In the course of one of these out-of-town excursions I came upon the village of Pokrovskoye, where Rasputin was born and lived before his meteoric rise through the high society of St Petersburg. The village's older inhabitants remembered the famous faith healer. They told me that before he became a holy man he was regarded as a layabout, a rake and a horse-thief. That was why he was called Rasputin, they said: *rasputstvo* in Russian means "debauchery". They also recalled that when Tsarina Alexandra Fedorovna visited the village just before the First World War, the path to his house was covered with carpets.

At the end of 1943 a government commission led by Georgi

My father (fourth from left) and me (cut, far right) with members of the
government commission appointed to check the condition of the body while
it was at Tiumen in late 1942. Mardashev (second from right) was to
become director of the mausoleum after my father's arrest in 1952.

Miterev, People's Commissar for Health, visited Tiumen to inspect the body prior to the twentieth anniversary of Lenin's death the following January. After this latest inspection, the government awarded my father not only the Order of Lenin but also the supreme title of "Hero of Socialist Labour". I received the Order of the Red Flag of Labour.

Meanwhile, as the Western Allies advanced through France and the Low Countries into Germany, Soviet troops on the Eastern Front were pursuing the enemy on his own territory. We went to Moscow to make arrangements for the return of the body to the mausoleum. This operation duly took place in March 1945, just before the conquest and occupation of Berlin by Soviet troops.

IX

Berlin 1945

"Colonel Deborin got here first . . . "

Berlin, 15 May 1945. My head is crowded with images: blocks of houses reduced to heaps of rubble, bridges down, burned-out tanks. Refugees shoot at a little cart; a Russian soldier steals a German woman's bicycle; men kneel on the pavement to cut up a horse that has been shot; swarms of flies hover over putrefying corpses. The stench of death and desolation is everywhere.

"Fasanenstrasse?" I asked an old man dragging a big sack of potatoes along the ground. He nodded to me to carry on in the same direction as before. I jumped back in the car. Second on the left, third on the right. I ran my finger over the map Soviet HQ had supplied us with that morning. "Stop! This is it," I said to our driver, a Red Army soldier. Getting out of the back of the car I was met with the sight of a brick-built workshop lying in ruins, its frame still smoking. There was a notice on the door: "Merck and Co. New address: 17 Kurfürstendamm." "Again!" I raged. This was the fifth change of address we'd come across since we started trying to locate Merck and Co. We were beginning to think we'd never find that famous firm and the chemicals we needed.

The Kurfürstendamm address proved to be an old apartment

block. It was dark inside. The light switch produced no result, and the lift wasn't working. Several parts of the city had been without electricity since the beginning of May. We groped our way up the stairs. On the sixth floor we made out a scrap of white paper pinned on the wall; striking a match we read on it the word "Merck". Knocking at the door, we were confronted by a tall man going grey at the temples. "Merck and Co.?" I asked. "That's right," he said. Despite the devastation in the city all around him he was impeccably dressed in a tweed suit, gold and crimson tie, and English shoes of highly polished brown leather. "Do come in," he said, clicking his heels, and we followed him along a gloomy corridor and into a large drawing room.

"We're here", began Mardashev, "to collect some chemicals . . . " Merck's employee – if that was what he was – interrupted him. "I'm afraid you've come to the wrong place. This is only the office. You'll probably find what you want at our factory in Darmstadt." That was about twenty kilometres south of Frankfurt, in the Allied Zone. Much too far away. We could scarcely conceal our disappointment. I looked round the room to make sure the man was telling the truth. All I could see was a jumble of old paintings, oriental carpets, statuettes and silver candlesticks littering the floor. "You see what a terrible state the war has reduced us to!" exclaimed our host. "He thinks this is terrible," I thought to myself. "You can tell he's never set foot in the USSR!"

We biochemists – Mardashev, Nikolai Deumin and I – had been ordered to go to Germany, recently defeated and now occupied by Soviet and Western Allied forces, and requisition all the chemicals and equipment the mausoleum laboratory might need. We were disguised for the purpose as Red Army officers; Mardashev was supposed to be a full colonel, while Deumin and I wore lieutenant-colonels' uniforms. We had been instructed to start collecting our booty in the western sector of Berlin, as that part of the city was soon to be handed over to the Western Allies. We had been given five weeks in which to carry out our depredations, we had at our disposal a few marks, a driver, and a car confiscated from a German.

After our fruitless pursuit of Merck and Co. we turned our attention to Dahlem, a suburb in the south-western part of Berlin where the Max-Planck Institute for Cell Physiology was. The institute had one of the most famous biochemistry laboratories in the world, and we were practically sure we'd find a veritable treasure trove of rare chemicals, microscopes, centrifuges, colorimeters, spectrometers, photometers, polarimeters and so on. When we got there we asked the caretaker what had become of Otto Warburg, the celebrated biochemist, physiologist and Nobel laureate who had been the director of the laboratory. "He doesn't work here any more," we were told. "He's a quarter Jewish [*Vierteljude*], you see, and banned from working in the Berlin area. He's living at Löwenburg now, a small place 35 kilometres away." We were rather relieved to hear this: at least Warburg wouldn't have to witness the dreadful spectacle of us looting his lab. Here again, however, we were in for disappointment. The laboratory had been completely gutted. "A fellow countryman of yours, Colonel Deborin, got here first," a young German scientist told us sadly. "He came yesterday and took everything."

We then hurried to the University of Berlin[38] on the Unter den Linden in the city's centre, where the fighting had been fiercest. Its façade was blackened by fire and pocked with bullet strikes. When we knocked at the door of the biochemistry department, however, we received the same reply as before: "Colonel Deborin got here first." We were furious. The hunt had only been on for a week, and we were already being left behind! Gavriil Deborin, our rival, was pillaging on behalf of the Institute of Biochemistry, where he was Director of Research, helped by the fact that he had friends among the heads of the Russian Academy of Sciences. Nor were we in any position to object to his methods, for we were doing the same thing ourselves.

For the next few days we decided to increase our chances of success by splitting up and searching separately. Mardashev kept the car and the driver, while Deumin and I walked or used public transport. The Berliners had taken only a few days to get the buses and metro going again, and as I made my way all over the city I was struck by the docility and discipline of the people. Often we could hear a strange kind of buzz in the streets, a rhythmical hiss rather like the sound of a steam engine. Men, women, children and even old people had formed chains and were passing buckets of rubble from hand to hand in order to clear the roadways. Every time anyone held out a bucket he or she said "Bitte schön", to which the other person would answer "Danke schön", hence the curious murmur. One day in the metro I heard an old woman complaining loudly about the galloping inflation and food shortages. Some Soviet officers were in the same compartment, though they couldn't understand what she said. Nevertheless the other German passengers became indignant and told her to keep quiet. "You should be ashamed, showing your countrymen up like that!" they chided her.

The workers in the chemical factories we went to reflected the same sort of resignation as they wrapped up the supplies we had requisitioned, carefully packing the chemicals into cartons to avoid mishaps. The same could not be said of the Ukrainian girls to whom we had at first entrusted the task. In spite of our instructions they managed to pack the phials upside down, with the result that some corrosive acids leaked out. Those young women had clearly failed to unlearn the methods current in the USSR.

In truth, however, the Germans' docility was motivated mainly by fear. "Is it true the Mongols will soon be in Berlin and that everything will be even worse than it is now?" one worried old woman asked me.[39] And, naturally, all the destruction – the ruined houses and wrecked streets – was the work of the Tommies, the British. "You Russians couldn't have done that," the Berliners would tell us.

Although acts of resistance were rare, I did witness one. Mardashev and I decided one day to go and inspect the German army's medical academy. At least, we thought, Colonel Deborin would not have thought of venturing there. At the end of a long corridor we were greeted by an extraordinary sight: a huge room with a mountain of Wehrmacht uniforms piled up in the middle. We realized this must have been where German soldiers came to get rid of their gear in the hope of saving their skins. Just as we were about to leave we caught sight of a German officer at the other end of the corridor, holding a pistol. He immediately fired, but we had managed to shelter behind a wall. Then came the sound of someone running in heavy boots, followed by the slamming of a door. I peered out into the corridor. No one there. Apparently the officer had taken fright, but we had had a narrow escape. When we got back to headquarters and described what had happened we were told we must never go about the city again without carrying revolvers.

The apprehensions of the Germans about the 'Red Hordes' were not, unfortunately, wholly groundless, for they derived in part from the sometimes less than admirable behaviour of our own troops. Many thirsty Red Army soldiers plundered the cellars of hotels and restaurants, knocking back the contents of any bottles they could lay hands on, and this naturally led to a number of tragic incidents. One day Marshadev and I visited a military hospital, and found there several of our soldiers complaining of having lost their sight. When we asked the doctor on duty about this he said, "They drank methyl alcohol from a laboratory – they sniffed at the bottles but couldn't tell the difference."

This kind of barbaric behaviour disgusted the Berliners. Once, when I was on a tram going to our headquarters in Karlhorst, a suburb in the south-east of Berlin, I was struck by the noble appearance of one of the woman passengers. She had brownish hair, a finely carved profile, widely spaced dark grey eyes and an ivory complexion, and she bore herself proudly. As I was admiring her a squadron of Soviet tanks charged, in utter disorder, into the street we were in, their great steel tracks seeming to devour the cobblestones. Soldiers perching on the turrets brandished bottles and shouted bawdy songs. The tanks tore up everything in their path – traffic lights, bus shelters, a garden hedge. I turned to look at the beautiful stranger. Tears were pouring down her lovely face.

Despite such examples of misbehaviour, however, and despite orders forbidding fraternization, there were innumerable romances between Russian soldiers and German girls, although this clearly had something to do with the shortage of German men, for millions of them had died in action, or in the Allied bombing. Indeed, I myself got to know a young German girl. It happened while our search was targeted on the north-eastern suburbs of Berlin. Deumin was with me that day, and as we were going through the park at Weissensee our eyes were caught by the slim figures of a couple of girls. One was tall and fair, the other of medium height with chestnut hair. We asked them the way, and learned that their names were Helga and Ursula.

I was very struck by Helga's looks. She was beautiful, with a high, rounded forehead, almond-shaped light grey eyes, diaphanous blue-veined temples, a nose like that of a Greek goddess and neat cherry-red lips. As she gave us directions in her fluting voice, she kept pushing away from the corner of her mouth a wayward lock of hair that always sprang back again.

Delighted at this unexpected encounter, we arranged for the four of us to meet on the following day and go to Lake Tegel. Once there, Deumin and Ursula walked in front, with Helga and me a few paces behind. I asked her what it had been like to be at school under Hitler. She said that she had been made to swallow large doses of the "foundations of national socialism" and "racial theory", subjects she and her schoolmates all detested. This struck me as strangely familiar, for it reminded me of the "social science" and "history of the Party" that we had been forced to study in the USSR.

Probably as a gesture of defiance, Helga had read the works of authors banned by the Nazis. "Come to my place," she said after our third meeting, "and I'll show you the books I saved from the burning. I kept them in a secret hiding place." The house Helga lived in was in Nieder Schönhausen, a north-eastern suburb of Berlin. Going back at night to Soviet headquarters on the other side of the city was a complicated business, since the public transport was not yet back to normal. So Helga invited me to stay the night. On that first visit we read Heine's poems and translations of Gogol together till late into the night.

She lived with her mother in a two-storey cottage about which, strangely, I can recall very little, except that the windowpanes had been blown out by the explosions of bomb or shells. Helga's mother was a Berliner of French extraction, who up till then had always been a housewife. Her husband, a manager, had died in the war, leaving her a few savings that had melted away because of the rapid devaluation of the mark and galloping inflation. As a result it had become very difficult for the two women to feed themselves.

Food supplies in Berlin had gradually improved, however. The black market flourished around the Brandenburg Gate, where a motley crowd speaking French, Polish, Dutch, Romany or Ukrainian peddled all sorts of wares – a few shrivelled apples, a sallow chicken, some dried fish, bottles of beer. These were people who had been deported from their own countries to perform forced labour in Germany, and who were now waiting in their hundreds of thousands to be repatriated.

Besides the black market, since 20 May some shops had been opened specially for the use of the Soviet armed forces. In them we could get various kinds of cheese, ham, bacon, oranges, wine and so on – all of them very hard to come by in Moscow. We paid for them in "Occupation marks", money printed and issued under an Allied agreement in an attempt to control, or at least curb, some of Germany's financial and economical problems. In fact, these square notes had merely accelerated the inflation. Even so, they were for the time being good enough for my purposes, and I would go back to Helga's in the evening laden with food. One day, while I was having a meal with her and her mother there was a loud knocking at the door. It was a second lieutenant of the Red Army, who announced that his commanding officer wished to billet himself there. I told him in no uncertain terms that I was already staying there myself, and that there wasn't room for two. When I showed him my insignia as a lieutenant-colonel – a rank superior to that of his CO – the young officer gave in, not suspecting for a moment that my uniform was only a kind of fancy dress.

The commanding officer in question probably had designs on Helga himself. During one of the nights I spent with her she told me that on 1 May, soon after Soviet troops entered Berlin, a Russian officer had held a pistol to her mouth and raped her. I was shattered. "Did you only agree to sleep with me because I'm one of the victors?" I asked. "No, of course not," she said, gazing at me with her grey-blue eyes. "I like you."

Helga was eighteen. I was thirty-two, and very much in love with her. As I followed her long ash-blonde mane on our walks through the twists and turns of ruined Berlin, she seemed to me like some unattainable Valkyrie. She took me to the places that had been part of her childhood: her grandparents' house, the church she used to attend on Sundays, her school. But most of the buildings had been bombed out of existence.

One evening as we were walking in the Schlosspark we were suddenly blinded by the lights of an army truck, and before we had time to get out of the way a number of Soviet soldiers pinned us against the truck and started to search us. A lieutenant said to me: "Caught red-handed fraternizing with a German girl, Comrade Lieutenant-Colonel!" He took us to headquarters, where they had no difficulty identifying me. "Let me tell you," a general warned, "that if you do it again you could get a long prison sentence." "All I did was ask the girl the way," I answered innocently. "You may go – this once," he replied, giving me back my papers.

My time in Berlin was coming to an end. I was unhappy at the thought of parting from Helga, but, having no choice, I told her I was going back to Russia. She gave me a photograph of herself and wrote some verses in German on the back – a *Schlager* or popular song:

> *Zum Abschied reich ich dir die Hände*
> *Und sag'ganz leis: "Auf Wiedersehn."*
> *Ein schönes Märchen geht zu Ende*
> *Doch war so schön.*
>
> *Ich will dein Bild im Herzen tragen.*
> *Du weisst wie gernich ich bei dir blieb,*
> *Denn, will ich dir zum Abschied sagen:*
> *"Ich habe dich so lieb."*

> As we part I hold out my hands
> And whisper "Au revoir".
> A beautiful story is ending –
> A really lovely story.
>
> I'll keep your image in my heart.
> You know how I'd like to stay with you,
> And that's why as we part I tell you
> How dear you are to me.

After I'd packed my case I waited by the door. Helga didn't come, and I became worried. "What's the matter?" I asked her mother. "Sie weint [she's crying]." I rushed to her room and kissed her tenderly.

I kept her photograph carefully until 1952. By then, however, a new wave of terror was sweeping across the USSR, and I realized that the German words written on the back of the picture might be compromising. In the end I decided to tear it up. Nor do I know what became of Helga after we parted. Perhaps she became an actress in the United States, which was what she had wanted to do. She had some Jewish friends who had emigrated there in the 1930s and had offered to help her. In 1973 I was invited to East Berlin for a symposium on the biochemistry of erythrocytes (red blood cells), and Professor Rapoport of Humboldt University (as the University of Berlin had been renamed) asked me to stay with him. He lived in the same neighbourhood as Helga had done, and I wandered for hours around Nieder Schönhausen looking for her house. But in vain.

By the middle of June 1945, having visited all the relevant companies and laboratories in Berlin, we had collected the supplies we needed. We still had to find a way of getting our "trophies" back to Moscow, however. Nikolai Deumin and I went to the freight office at the station, where we found a crowd of Russian officers haranguing the dispatch clerk. Being inferior to them in rank, he put up with their insults stoically. The rule seemed to be that the officer who bawled the loudest was the one most likely to be allocated a truck to take his war trophies home. Deumin and I, unused to behaving so offensively, came a long way last in this game.

Next day Deumin had another try. He plunged boldly into the scrum and after half an hour returned looking triumphant. Surprised by his success, I asked, "Were you rude to the dispatch clerk too?" No, he said. On the contrary he'd been very courteous, and the man had said to him: "You're the first person who's spoken to me politely. Before the war I was a judge. People spoke to me differently then. I'll let you have a truck." Accordingly, test-tubes, chemicals, microscopes, photometers, centrifuges, electric pumps and all sorts of other equipment were piled one on top of the other on a train for Moscow. We looked forward to doing good work with such excellent equipment, although for some time we felt rather guilty towards our German counterparts. What we had done in Berlin that year had been neither ethical nor decent.

Unfortunately, because I was still in Germany in June 1945, I was unable to attend the great victory parade in Moscow that month. This I greatly regretted, for I was told that it was by far the most moving ceremony Red Square had ever seen. Friends and acquaintances who were there, however, gave me a detailed description of it.

Red Square was shrouded in mist on the morning of 24 June, and it started to rain just before the march-past began. "Heaven is weeping for our dead," remarked one of the Muscovites gathered near the Kremlin. The best soldiers from all the ten Red Army 'fronts' (army groups) were drawn up in columns opposite the mausoleum. On the stroke of ten o'clock the band struck up Glinka's famous *Slavsia* march. Heading the procession, Marshal Zhukov was the first to appear in Red Square, mounted on his tall white charger. He rode past the ranks of soldiers, who cheered in answer to their leader's salute. Zhukov spoke later of how moved he had been, and that he had seemed to see all the men who had died in action filing past him.

The ceremony had been carefully rehearsed the previous day. Among other preparations a special detachment of soldiers chosen for their height had practised throwing staves outside the mausoleum. A few hours before the ceremony these gathered at St Basil's Cathedral, where each man was entrusted with the standard of a German division. "Here, take Hitler's private standard," a general said to a particularly burly soldier. The man, seeing Hitler's name and a large swastika surrounded by a laurel wreath and surmounted by an eagle at the top of the staff, drew back, thinking that to touch such an object might bring bad luck. "Take it," said the general." It's the most prestigious of them all." The soldier took it.

After riding round the square, Zhukov dismounted, climbed the steps of the mausoleum, and went to stand beside Stalin on the rostrum. Then the 200 men of the special detachment began hurling the standards of the German divisions to the ground, to the accompaniment of drum rolls.

Emotion reached its height. Party officials, generals and admirals had tears in their eyes. Marshal Budenny, a hero of the Civil War who was thought to be a bit simple, was still standing at attention; he had not realized that it was quite unsuitable to salute the colours of a vanquished army. Despite the jubilation, however, there was a more cautious note. A cordon of very tall guards had been placed in front of the mausoleum to prevent any of the soldiers from aiming one of the enemy standards at the General Secretary of the Party. The parade lasted nearly two hours, marred only by the bad weather, which made a fly-past impossible.

Meanwhile, underneath the mausoleum, the surroundings in which Lenin's body lay had undergone some changes. The corpse had been brought back to Moscow in March 1945 by the same special train on which it had travelled to Tiumen, its journey entirely uneventful. As the body had received rejuvenation treatment while it was at Tiumen, the government decided to reward our efforts. The mausoleum laboratory, of which my father had been made the director in 1939, was given new and larger premises. Moreover, under the same roof were also installed the department of biological and analytical chemistry

The sarcophagus in 1945, rearranged after Lenin's body was brought back to Moscow.

of the Moscow First Medical Institute, and the biochemistry laboratory of the Institute of Oncology, both of which were also directed by my father.

Lenin's sarcophagus, which had hitherto been cone-shaped, had now been replaced by one in the form of an inverted trapezium, an arrangement which eliminated reflections from the glass sides. The lighting, too, was much improved, for the intensity could now be regulated by means of fixtures inside the upper part of the catafalque.[40] So far as realism went, the face and hands of the corpse, which had been very pale before our work during the war, had taken a pinker, and thus more lifelike, tone.

X

The Dictatorship of the Party in Matters of Science

"The Rasputin of science"

The equipment we had commandeered in Germany enabled us to make some scientific breakthroughs in the study of cellular nuclei. These advances produced important repercussions in the international scientific community, with the result that requests for offprints of accounts of our researches came in from all over the world. Unfortunately, however, it had become impossible to send them, for the "Iron Curtain" had come down. Mistrust of foreigners was at its height. All one ever heard about was the "military genius" of Stalin and the "superiority of the Russian people and Russian culture".

Nor was science immune from the nationalistic frenzy. Merely referring to the researches of foreign scientists was regarded as suspect. All important discoveries were attributed to Soviet scientists, or to Russian scientists if the discoveries in question dated from before the Revolution. Furthermore, portraits and busts of world-famous figures like Newton, Pasteur and Helmholtz[41] were removed from some provincial universities and institutes. We were completely cut off from the rest of the world.

An eminent Japanese scientist who took a close interest in our researches asked several times if he might have an account of them. To send him one, however, we needed the permission of the Minister of Health. Debov, a new colleague of mine, offered to take care of the necessary formalities, but when he went to the ministry no one would listen to him. The following day he tried again, with the result that the head of the foreign department finally agreed to see him.

The first thing Debov was asked was whether he knew the Japanese scientist's political affiliations. "Is he a conservative? a liberal? a socialist?" said the official with inquisitorial severity. "I don't know," he answered. "All I know is that he's a great scientist." "Well, if you really want to send him what he asks for," this bureaucrat declared, "write out a detailed report on his life, his scientific career, and his attitude towards the USSR." Debov, of course, was careful not to do any such thing. It would have been much too risky.

The Institute of Oncology, where I began to work after the war, circulated confidential instructions to its staff. The document contained eleven paragraphs, but could be summarized in one sentence: "Talking to foreigners is forbidden." If a foreigner was taken ill or suffered a minor accident, we were not allowed to offer him medical aid without the permission of the Ministry of Health. Only in the case of a serious accident, read the last paragraph of the circular, could a foreigner be treated without first gaining previous official authorization.

The elation that followed the announcement of victory over Germany had made me hope for some relaxation of the terror. The streets of Moscow offered the unusual spectacle of women, children and soldiers embracing one another, dancing or weeping for joy. Fireworks had been let off over the Moskva, watched by masses of people packing the bridges. I can still see the American Ambassador waving from his balcony to the jubilant crowd. The intensity of the Russian people's joy reflected the immense sacrifice the country had made in terms of human lives. Twenty million dead – more than all the other European countries put together.

Even during the war we had been given some reason to believe that there had been a degree of liberalization. It was a time when the boldest citizens had not hesitated to say what they thought. I remember meeting a colonel on a train who complained about the fact that generals and other senior officers were allowed to inflict corporal punishment on non-commissioned officers. That, he said, had never been the case in the Tsarist army.

There was also some rehabilitation of the Orthodox religion during the war years. Before 1941 it was regarded as dangerous to go into a church or even to cross oneself. Between the early 1920s and the beginning of the war, thousands of priests were executed or sent to forced labour camps. Some 90 per cent of the churches, including a number of magnificent cathedrals, were destroyed or converted into garages or agricultural depots. At the outbreak of hostilities with Germany, however, Stalin, a former seminarian, realized that it would be in his, and the state's, interest to rehabilitate religion as a means of helping to unite the country against the invader. Repression against priests ceased, and many churches were reopened to the public.

In the summer of 1945, when Stalin and the Allied leaders were meeting in Potsdam to discuss the future of Europe, I was naive enough to think that an agreement with the Western Powers would inevitably lead to a democratization of our own regime, of which we had, I thought, seen early signs during the war.

Churchill's announcement of the beginning of the Cold War in June 1947 put an end to my illusions, however.

Nor was nationalism the only marked characteristic of Stalin's post-war policy, for the period was also one of extreme ideological repression, in scientific as in other fields. After the dropping of the American-built atom bombs on Hiroshima and Nagasaki, Stalin suddenly woke up to the backwardness of Soviet science. In this, he was forgetting that it was he who, just before the war, had ordered the Academy of Sciences to halt its researches into the nucleus of the atom because they had "no practical usefulness for the socialist economy".

Stalin now sent for Sergei Vavilov, the President of the Academy, and asked him what needed to be done to bridge the scientific gap between the USSR and the United States. Vavilov replied that one measure was a matter of urgency: scientists' salaries must be increased. As a result, the earnings of qualified scientists were quadrupled.

Our family benefited greatly from this sudden revaluation of science. My father, as director of the mausoleum laboratory and professor of biochemistry at the First Medical Institute, as well as head of the biochemistry laboratory at the Institute of Oncology, was from then on earning 1,800 roubles a month – more than a member of the Central Committee of the Party. The sudden increase in his salary barely affected his lifestyle, however. He still enjoyed the same privileges as before the war: access to the special shops reserved for the nomenklatura, a five-room apartment opposite the Kremlin, a car, a dacha.

I myself now earned 600 roubles a month, enough to feed and clothe my small family adequately. By this time I was a married man, and since 1947 the father of a little boy, Alexei; another

Myself in 1947, recently promoted to head the biochemistry lab at the Institute of Oncology. My wife, Irina, and I enjoyed a very pleasant and prosperous lifestyle. My first son, Alexei, was born that year.

son, Dimitri, was to follow in 1952. We lived in a three-room flat overlooking Tsvetnoi Boulevard in the middle of Moscow, a modestly furnished apartment with a few plywood beds, tables and chairs in the Soviet style of the day. The years of real hardship seemed to have gone for ever.

Left to right: my wife Irina, myself, my father, my half-brothers Victor and Felix and their mother, my father's second wife, Eugenie, in 1947.

As I have said, my father took up his new job as head of the biochemistry laboratory at the Institute of Oncology in 1945. In actual fact, however, he was so absorbed in his other activities that he practically never set foot there. I was the one who really did his work, although that did not stop him from collecting the salary. I was more or less "ghosting" for him, and it was not until 1946 that I officially replaced him and was appointed head of the biochemistry lab.

Not surprisingly, I was very glad of the promotion, not only because of the increased salary, but also because it allowed me at last to break free from my father's influence. I did not share his ideas about biochemistry, and the research he had made me do into the transmission of amino acids by red blood cells and the

My father in 1947. At the time he held several high-ranking positions concurrently, and was amongst the privileged few. He believed that our family would not be affected by the purges.

influence of amino acids on the growth of tumours had produced very meagre results. "You don't really respect me as a scientist," he said to me one day. I demurred, but he wouldn't believe me. It is true, however, that I did think he spent much too much time making up to pen-pushing ministers, much to the detriment of his scientific work. One result of our different outlooks was that a certain amount of jealousy mingled with his pride when he learned of the important discoveries Sergei Debov and I had made.

Thanks partly to the materials we had commandeered in Berlin, we had managed to divide the nuclei of cells derived from a number of different tissues and tumours. The fractions we had obtained in our researches had never been observed before, and our work showed that the residue from the nucleus was essential to the total metabolism of the cell. Even today biochemists studying cellular nuclei, including those in foreign countries, always mention the pioneer work we did then.

I had met Sergei Debov soon after the war, when, still in the uniform of an officer of the Red Army, he came to my office. He had trained as a doctor, but told me he was specially interested in the biochemistry of cancer. Impressed by his intelligence and self-control, I asked him to come and work with me in the biochemistry lab at the Institute, an offer which he accepted at once. At twenty-six he was seven years my junior, and he obviously had a great future. As it turned out, however, our research was to be interrupted by the growing influence of "Lysenkoism" on science in the Soviet Union.

Trofim Denisovitch Lysenko was a plant biologist and agronomist born in Karlova, in the Ukraine, in 1898. His only intellectual qualification was a secondary-school leaving certificate from an agricultural college, though this didn't stop him seeing himself as a great scientist. In 1938, thanks to the eminent biologist Nikolai Vavilov (the elder brother of Sergei Vavilov, future President of the Academy of Sciences), Lysenko took part in a scientific conference, and this marked the beginning of his irresistible rise towards the pinnacles of power. At that conference he caused a sensation by claiming that heredity did not work through genes (as Mendel had proposed, in laws that have to come to form the basis of modern genetics), but that both plants and humans owed their development wholly to their environment.

Lysenko's theory flew in the face of the laws established by modern biology, and a lively debate followed at the Academy of Agricultural Sciences. Lysenko said he agreed with "Michurin's biology"[42], which postulated the theory that acquired characteristics are heritable, and that the behaviour of plants is therefore determined by natural forces and environmental influences. Since Lysenko was merely a Russian agronomist who, probably through ignorance, displayed scant respect for the laws of biology, his theories ought to have carried little weight. None the less, the Central Committee of the Party decided in favour of his ideas, and he was elected a member of the Academy of Agricultural Sciences. His chief detractor, Nikolai Vavilov, President of that institution and the man who had brought Lysenko to the 1938 conference, was arrested and sent to prison, where he died in 1942.

It is alleged that one of the reasons for Lysenko's growing power in the world of science was his ability to act upon people's subconscious, thanks to certain "mysterious fluids". Certainly he was to become a kind of Rasputin of science. Although nothing was heard of him during the war years, he rose to the surface again in 1948. In an article in the *Literaturnaya Gazeta* he confidently asserted that there was no struggle for survival between members of the same species. The article provoked some caustic comments from leading biologists, and the *Gazeta* went on to publish the views of several famous experts for whom Lysenko's ideas clearly lacked any scientific foundation. Nevertheless, the journal concluded that Lysenko had won the argument.

The Dean of the faculty of biology at the University of Moscow, Yudintsev, had other ideas, however. He organized a discussion to demonstrate the absurdity of Lysenko's theories. Lysenko refused to take part, although his presence would probably not have influenced the outcome, for the meeting unanimously rejected his ideas. Nevertheless, Yudintsev realized that he had only won a battle; to win the war he must obtain the support of Yuri Zhdanov, head of the Science Department of the Party's Central Committee. Zhdanov did come down on the side of the Dean, although not before he had consulted his father, Andrei Zhdanov, the powerful Politburo member in charge of ideology.

In August 1948 a plenary meeting of the Academy of Agricultural Sciences examined Lysenko's theories, and once again they were demolished by his colleagues. Their author, however, brought the debate to an end by declaring that Stalin had sided with him. It was not an idle boast. The Kremlin had indeed just made Lysenko President of the Academy of Agricultural Sciences and an active member of the Soviet Academy of Sciences. As a result, the younger Zhdanov had to make a public apology in *Pravda*. (It is interesting to note that his father died of a heart attack at almost the same time.) Some well-known biologists and members of the Academy of Agricultural Sciences were imprisoned; others committed suicide rather than accept Lysenko's theories. A number of famous laboratories were closed.

The Director of the Institute of Oncology sent for me and

told me that we were to drop our research into cellular nuclei immediately. To study that subject implied a belief in the highly bourgeois notion of heredity, and an acceptance of the contemptible tradition of "Mendelism-Weismannism-Morganism". The Austrian monk, botanist and biologist Gregor Mendel (1822–84), the German biologist August Weismann (1834–1914), and the American geneticist and biologist Thomas Morgan (1866–1945) were (and still are) regarded as the founding fathers of modern genetics. Since Michurin's theories had been adopted as official doctrine, however, the mere mention of these pioneers' names was regarded as an insult to the authorities and could result in the direst consequences. Thus Lysenko's ravings were incorporated into official doctrine and became the tablets of the law not only for us in Russia but for all Communist Parties throughout the world.

In 1949, while on an official visit to Bulgaria, I happened to meet the General Secretary of the Belgian Communist Party. I asked him for news of Jean Brachet, a famous Belgian biologist whom I had come to know a year and a half earlier. "Professor Brachet", said the Belgian, "may be a member of the Party but he is not a true Marxist." I asked him why not. "Because," he replied with some annoyance, "when I asked him if he agreed with the Party's official policy towards biology, he said, 'I don't know, I'll have to think about it.'" Such hesitation was, it seems, unforgivable, and as a result Comrade Brachet had become an object of suspicion within his own party.

Even after Stalin's death in 1953, Lysenko's grip on Soviet science did not slacken, for Khrushchev continued to invite him to take part in plenary sessions of the Central Committee. Nevertheless, at one of these meetings the new General Secretary of the Party, struck by Lysenko's crass ignorance, remarked: "I can see how a peasant might talk like a scholar, but that an academician can talk like a peasant – I can't understand that at all!"

From 1957 on, however, Lysenko and his followers were subjected to a barrage of criticism. *Pravda* published a violent attack on an article by one of Lysenko's colleagues in the periodical *Agrobiologie*, which had described a series of experiments apparently demonstrating the metamorphosis of a pine tree into a fir. *Pravda* maintained that no such transformation ever took place: branches of fir had simply been grafted on to the pine tree. Yet once again Lysenko managed to wriggle out of the difficulty.

The discovery of the genetic code by a team of American scientists made Khrushchev aware of how far Soviet biology lagged behind. President Kennedy had declared that in physics the Soviets were practically neck and neck with the Americans, but that in the field of biology the USSR still had a long way to go to catch up. After that speech, Khrushchev ordered the immediate creation of a Council for Molecular Biology, and I was made one of its active members. Most of my colleagues on the council agreed to recognize the established principles of modern biology, rather than those of Lysenkoism.

The Chairman of the council, Vladimir Engelhardt, made a speech to the presidium of the Academy of Sciences about the state of research in molecular biology. During the meeting Ivan Knuniants, a chemist of Armenian extraction, remarked ironically: "When I pick up the great Soviet encyclopedia and look up the word 'gene' the physical transmitter of heredity, what do I find? That the idea is only a myth. A myth, do you hear? The pupils in our schools are taught that so-called modern biology is mere Darwinism and a load of rubbish."

Lysenko, who, as a member of the Academy, was also present, hardly let Knuniants finish his sentence. In his grating voice he said that a transcription of the latter's remarks absolutely must be published in the newspapers. At first I failed to understand what he was driving at. Then a woman journalist sitting beside me whispered, "Don't you see? When the papers print that 'Darwinism is a load of rubbish' Lysenko will have the Academy of Sciences where he wants it." Since Darwinism had been adopted as a doctrine by the Communists, one was not permitted to criticize it.

Crafty as he might be, Lysenko could not always conceal his extraordinary ignorance. Andrei Belozersky, a biochemist who had been elected to the Academy of Sciences for his work on nucleic acids, told me of a conversation he had had with Lysenko. The latter had invited Belozersky to come to his own Institute of Genetics to tell him and his colleagues about nucleic acids, the chemical substances that are the physical carriers of genes and thus of heredity.

When Belozersky had finished speaking, Lysenko's colleagues waited to hear their chief's reaction. "Seeing that the chemists have discovered nucleic acids," he declared solemnly, "that means they must exist and chemists must study them. What I would like, my dear Professor, is for you to show me this deoxyribonucleic acid ... " He had difficulty pronouncing the long word, so familiar to biologists. Belozersky invited him to his laboratory to examine the acid, but Lysenko politely declined, saying, "Send me the deoxyribonucleic acid in a jar." A few days later Belozersky sent him some in a test tube. Lysenko looked at it doubtfully. "Is it really deoxyribonucleic acid?" he asked. He was told it was. "But why isn't it liquid, then?" he asked, obviously ignorant of the fact that an acid may exist in solid form. It was quite inadmissible that anyone at that level of the scientific hierarchy should make such a gross blunder, yet Lysenko was never chastised.

"Michurin's biology", established by Lysenko as official Party doctrine in that field, had parallels in other branches of science. One example of this was to be seen in the state's attitude to the work of the physiologist and Nobel laureate Ivan Pavlov, who discovered the conditioned reflex. This materialistic conception of the functioning of the brain fitted in perfectly with the views of the Party, and was therefore elevated into a dogma which precluded any physiological research that might challenge it. For all that, Pavlov was undoubtedly a great scientist, and his researches undeniably of scientific value.

The same could not be said, however, of some other "innovators" who, taking Lysenko as their example, introduced discoveries each more far-fetched than the last. In the late 1940s, not long before the beginning of the Cold War, when relations between the Allies and the USSR were still relatively cordial, the microbiologist Nina Klueva and the histologist Grigory Roskin announced that they had just discovered a new treatment for cancer based on *Trypanosoma cruzi*, a protozoan (single-celled) blood parasite from South America.

The announcement caused a sensation. The Americans were the first to react. General Walter Bedell Smith, the United States Ambassador in Moscow, contacted those who laid claim to the discovery. "It concerns the whole human race," he said. "I should like our two countries to sign an agreement to combine our researches." The Soviet official in charge of the state's anti-cancer programme, informed of the American interest, referred at once to the Ministry of Health. In turn the Minister, M.A. Miterev, having received a verbal go-ahead from the Central Committee, instructed his staff to draw up a draft agreement.

When Stalin found out that the Minister of Health intended to pass on to the Americans a "discovery" made by Soviet science he went mad with rage. He ordered the arrest of the official in the anti-cancer department, and of all those involved in preparing the draft agreement. The scientific secretary of the presidium of the Academy of Medical Sciences was arrested and sentenced to fifteen years in prison: it was he who had taken Roskin and Klueva's book, *The Biotherapy of Cancer*, to America. Miterev was removed from his post and made to appear, together with the two scientists responsible for the "discovery", before a "court of honour". I was present at that court, and saw Miterev, Roskin and Klueva accused of high treason, lack of patriotism, and "cosmopolitanism". I remember that one of the charges against Roskin was that he had accepted the gift of a pen from a foreigner.

From now on, cancer research became the subject of constant surveillance. The publication or dissemination of any "research that was not completely finished" was forbidden. This decree naturally produced a wave of panic in the scientific community, since in general it is very rare for any scientific research to be "completely finished".

There were, however, other innovators who, stimulated by Roskin and Klueva's "discoveries", racked their brains for new methods of treating cancer. Some suggested that patients should eat the fungi that grow on birch trees; others recommended the buds of certain tropical shrubs. One day one of these people went to see the surgeon A.I. Savitsky, Director of the Institute of Oncology, and calmly suggested that he treat his patients by dressing them in garments made of radioactive material.

Savitsky, though no theoretician, saw through this fraud at once, and had his staff show the charlatan the door. Next day, however, Savitsky was summoned by the Minister of Health, who rebuked him for not being "constructive" and ordered him to try out the radioactive clothing idea in his institute. Needless to say, the results of the tests were negative.

Most of the "innovators" were protected by Lysenko and the chief Party authorities, as was demonstrated in the case of the elderly Bolshevik, Olga Lepechinskaya. After observing egg yolks through a microscope, she came to the conclusion that this "living matter" produced cells. Such an idea was completely contrary to the observations of Pasteur, among others, and this "scientific revolution" was almost unanimously dismissed by eminent scientists both in the USSR and abroad. Even so, that did not stop Olga Lepechinskaya being elected, with Lysenko's support, to membership of the Medical Academy. Moreover, it became compulsory for her work on egg yolks, like Michurin's biology, to be studied in all the biology departments in the USSR.

As if all this were not enough, Lysenko's imitators included some dangerous madmen, a number of whom I had occasion to meet. One, an army officer, had been warmly recommended to me by a friend. He too claimed to have found a panacea for cancer, in his case salts of uranium. He showed me a pile of enthusiastic letters from patients he had already treated by this method, and expressed the hope that I would give it my scientific backing. I declined, pointing out that uranium, as well as being radioactive, was also a heavy metal and as such a dangerous poison. He went away disgruntled. A few minutes later the friend whom he had got to recommend him burst into my office. "Ilya, what have you done?" he cried, looking very worried. I tried to explain that the "cure" in question was harmful, but he would not listen. "You've just missed out on making a lot of money," he told me.

It was certainly true that those responsible for "discoveries", and the scientists who backed them, could be very generously rewarded by the state, something which accounted for the appearance on the scene of researchers of all kinds. Among them there were certainly many crooks trying to take material advantage of the "boost" Stalin gave to science after the war, but there were also plenty of ignoramuses who truly believed their ideas were sound. The damage they did to Soviet science was irreparable, not least because eminent scholars wasted vasts amounts of time and energy demonstrating the absurdity of some of the new theories. Nevertheless, the situation was symptomatic of the increasing encroachment of politics upon the realm of science.

XI

My Father is Arrested

"Down with cosmopolitans!"

Early one morning in March 1952 I was in a wagon-lit on the Moscow-Leningrad train. Through the dawn mists I could see long lines of undulating hills, birch-fringed ravines, and the little grey villages so typical of our northern landscapes. Spring was just beginning and the days were getting longer, though the air had a wintry nip to it and the fields were still covered with snow. When I arrived in Leningrad I went to the Red Triangle factory, where every year I placed an order for the rubber bandages we used to prevent the "balsam" preserving Lenin's body from leaking away.

For some reason or other my trips to Leningrad almost always seemed to coincide with, for me, disagreeable incidents. I might, for instance, be greeted on my return to Moscow with the news that one of my sons had broken his arm, or that someone was ill, or that a friend had died. This time was no exception. When I returned from Leningrad I found my wife very worried. She told me my father had been arrested at his flat on 27 March.

The terror, which had never ceased since the early 1930s, had grown worse in the last few months. The regime was now targeting the "cosmopolitans", by which Stalin meant chiefly people of Jewish origin, who were accused of "Jewish national-ism" or "international Zionism". By a strange quirk of history, the Red Army's discovery in 1944 and 1945 of some of the Nazi concentration camps did not stop the Party from reappropriating the anti-Semitism of German fascism.

The death in 1948 of Salomon Mikhoels, the famous director of the Jewish Theatre in Moscow, marked the beginning of a wide-ranging anti-Semitic campaign. Mikhoels had been run over by a lorry in Minsk – or at least that was the official story as reported in the newspapers at the time. The body, of which the head and legs were badly mutilated, was brought to the mausoleum laboratory, where my father and Mardashev set about preparing it for the funeral. On examining it closely, however, they found evidence of a bullet wound, and naturally concluded that Mikhoels's death was not as "accidental" as the authorities would have everyone believe.

Stalin hated Mikhoels. As Chairman of the Jewish Anti-Fascist Committee, founded in 1941, the impresario had become the leader of the Jewish minority in the USSR. To a paranoid administration, that was cause enough for him to be suspected of spying for the American secret services, although there was never any proof to support the charge. After he was murdered the Jewish Anti-Fascist Committee was dismantled and most of its members arrested; its leaders were tried and executed in 1952.[43] Theatres and other artistic organizations were systematically purged. All the actors in the Jewish Theatre lost their jobs.

The campaign soon spread to the scientific sector. Special commissions were set up in ministries, scientific institutes and schools, with the object of eliminating all members of staff who were of dubious "nationality". I remember a decree issued by E.I. Smirnov, Minister of Health at the time, announcing the dismissal of M.P. Chumakovm, Director of the Poliomyelitis Institute, who had incautiously taken on staff from other institutions whose "professional and political qualifications" did not correspond with the Party line. The decree ended with a list of fifteen Jewish names. All these people were thrown out of work overnight, and left without any means of making a living.

Scientists of Jewish extraction were ruthlessly persecuted, no matter how senior or eminent. Jacob Oscar Parnas, the celebrated biochemist and Academician, was one example. Prior to 1939, he had been Professor of Chemical Biology in Lvov (a city which, as Lwów, had been Polish between the two wars), and had won a worldwide reputation for his work on glycolysis. After the signing in August 1939 of the Molotov-Ribbentrop Pact, however, which led to the annexation of eastern Poland by the USSR, Parnas was forced to go and work in Moscow, where he became a member of the Academy of Sciences and head of the Institute of Biological and Medical Chemistry. Unused to the devious behaviour of his Soviet colleagues, he treated them with some disdain, even those whose work made them his equals. Especially resented were the biology seminars he used to hold in his study, which were conducted in Russian spoken with a strong Polish accent, with comical mutilations of the language.

In the late 1940s Professor Parnas wrote a monograph in which he praised the superiority of black rye bread, rich in vitamins and minerals, over white bread made from wheat. He noted in support of his theory that in the Franco-Prussian war of 1870 the French, who ate bread made of wheat, were roundly defeated by the Prussians, who ate rye bread almost exclusively. He used the same argument to explain the superiority of the Soviets over the Nazis in the recent war.

The monograph, the publication of which coincided with the beginning of the campaign against the "cosmopolitans", provoked the wrath of Party dignitaries. Victory over the Nazi invader, they believed, had been brought about by the superiority of the USSR's political system, not by the ingredients of its people's food. Nor did Parnas's Jewish origins help his cause, and an order went out that he was to be detained. When the secret police who called for him told him he was about to be arrested, however, the shock was so great that he suffered a heart attack and died on the spot.

Other eminent Jewish scientists, like Lina Stern and Isaï Present suffered a similar fate. Lina Stern was for a long time greatly valued by the regime: she was one of the few foreign scientists who had decided to go and live in Russia after the October Revolution. Her special study was the nervous system, and she had led research into the haemato-encephalic barrier – the frontier between the blood and the cerebrospinal fluid – for which she had been elected an active member of the Academy of Sciences, although this did not prevent her arrest.

The case of Isaï Present was rather different. He was both a philosopher and a physiologist who, as a close colleague of Lysenko, used to brief the latter when he had to answer difficult scientific questions. We were very surprised when he was sent to prison, as his views coincided in every respect with the Party line. After these three arrests a saying, arguably in rather doubtful taste, began to circulate in Moscow: "Parnas is no longer a mountain, nor Stern a star, nor Present a gift."

These sinister events boded no good for my own family. I knew that as scientists of Jewish origin both my father and myself made ideal victims for the regime; we might lose our jobs and be arrested at any moment. My father, however, took things more philosophically. He thought our position as embalmers of Lenin and our reputation in the country in general would shield us from the worst eventualities. Then, in 1952, a year before Stalin's death, an ominous cloud began to hover over the mausoleum laboratory.

In February of that year – my father was ill at the time – I was sent with a small group of colleagues from the laboratory on a mission to Ulan Bator, capital of Mongolia, to embalm the body of the dictator Choybalsan. On the way back I was told by Sergei Debov that a commission from the Central Committee of the Party had come to inspect our laboratory with the purpose of uncovering any mistakes we might have made in our work on Lenin's body. We knew instinctively that the visit heralded trouble: whenever the Central Committee started such an inquiry a few heads could usually be expected to roll before it ended.

Back in Moscow we could see at once that our suspicions had been justified. Our offices had been turned upside down, drawers and cupboards searched. We scarcely spoke to one another any more for fear of saying something that could be held against us. We all knew that among us in the lab there must be *seksots*, secret collaborators whose job it was to report anything tendentious to the authorities. The MGB (which was succeeded by the MVD in 1953, and then by the KGB in 1954) had tens of thousands of spies working for it in companies, institutions and factories.

It was against this background, therefore, that I returned home from Leningrad towards the end of March 1952, to learn that my father had been arrested.

His imprisonment, which marked the beginning of very difficult times for our family, lasted nearly two years. We did not hear from him at all. We could neither write to him nor visit him. I was very worried and feared the worst. I also thought that the MGB would not delay in coming after me. The day after my father was arrested, I was indeed officially dismissed from the mausoleum laboratory on the grounds that I was not allowed to hold that position and at the same time be head of the laboratory at the Institute of Oncology, although I had held that post since 1946.

But that wasn't all: in the middle of April I was sacked from the Institute of Oncology. A commission from the Ministry of Health, acting on a Party directive, had decided that the managerial staff of all scientific institutes had to be selected on the basis of their "professional and political qualifications". This, in plain language, meant that Jews and the relatives of people who had been sent to prison were to be dismissed.

A few days later I was sent for by Boris Kazakov, head of the managerial department of the Russian Ministry of Health. He confirmed, although in a very sympathetic manner, that I had been dismissed from the Institute of Oncology. When I asked if he might be able to find me another post he became uncomfortable. "I know how competent and highly qualified you are", he said, "but unfortunately there's nothing I can do for you." Soviet society was divided into persecutors and victims. Within the first category, however, there was a new subdivision between those who enjoyed their evil work, and those who did it only reluctantly. In this sense, Kazakov was a decent man.

There were many scientists who, like me, found themselves out of work from one day to the next. There were even rumours in Moscow about deportation to the autonomous Jewish region of Birobidjan in the far east of Siberia. As for me, I couldn't find a job anywhere, not even as a caretaker or labourer. Both in

Moscow and in the provinces I came up against the same wall of suspicion. I tried to sell my books in order to keep body and soul together, but no bookseller was interested. My scientific articles were banned, and all references to my work in articles by my colleagues or pupils were systematically removed. My wife's meagre salary as a biology teacher in a medical school was not enough to feed our two children and us. My life, morally and physically, was soon a hell.

One day the MGB sent for me. The officers wanted to ask me questions about a gun I had received from the NKVD while in Tiumen. They did not believe that I had already given it back, although they eventually let me go. Before leaving, I tried to obtain through them some information about my father's health, and about his trial. When I asked them why he had been arrested, however, their answer was very depressing: "He's very guilty," they said.

Then I had another alarm. One night our doorbell rang at three in the morning. I feared the worst, certain that this time agents of the MGB had come to arrest me. When I opened the door, however, I could only laugh at my mistake. There stood Tsigankov, a neighbour who lived on the same landing, swaying tipsily and asking me to go and have a few vodkas with him at his place. I could not conceal the terrible fright he had given us.

Every day I waited for my arrest. I was constantly followed and my every move was watched. I went out as little as possible. Yet nothing ever happened, and I have only recently found out why. In Stalin's records, a secret file concerning my father and me has been found. Dated 1949 and written by Abakumov, head of the MGB at that time, it proposed the arrest of "Ilya and Boris Zbarsky, both guilty of counter-revolutionary conversations". A comment has been added in the margin in Stalin's hand, however: "Must not be touched until a substitute is found." As a result, my father was arrested somewhat later, in 1952, while I escaped imprisonment altogether.

The disasters that had befallen our family caused many friends and acquaintances to change their attitude towards us. When I talked about my professional problems to one of them on the telephone, he hung up immediately, and that was the last I heard of him. Another, a very old friend, crossed over when he saw me in the street. On the other hand, one friend – indeed, a mere acquaintance whom we'd seen only quite seldom before – now behaved very generously, offering us money and other material help. We were by now in such straits we were obliged to accept. Another acquaintance, a woman whom my wife knew, told us she worked for the MGB, and tried several times to intercede in our favour, albeit vainly.

My father was finally freed, "for lack of proof", on 30 December 1953. I was extremely surprised to learn that he had not heard of Stalin's death some eight months earlier, and had therefore failed to realize that he probably owed his freedom to that unforeseen event since otherwise he would have been kept in prison until he died. He had suffered terribly, and he emerged very thin and drawn, and with a cowed and nervous expression. I suggested he should go and rest for a while in a sanatorium, but he wouldn't hear of it. Anxious to get back to work, he found he was unable to get his job at the mausoleum back, and had to be satisfied with a post as second professor in the biochemistry department at the Moscow First Medical Institute.

News of the sudden death of the "father and best friend of the people", so completely unexpected by all save a handful, had plunged millions of Soviet men and women into a state of complete mental and emotional disarray. Conditioned by years of "political education", they had truly come to believe that Stalin was a great and good man, and that his ideas were both just and right. The disappearance of their guide left an enormous void in their lives for which they were quite unprepared. For my part, in the days following his death, the announcement that there was to be a government by "collective leadership" came as a relief to me. Dictatorship by a group, I thought, could not be as harsh as the despotism of one man.

The day before Stalin's funeral my wife and I went to Trubnaya Plochad, where a sea of people, their faces pale and their eyes filled with tears, was moving silently toward the House of Trade Unions where the corpse of the tyrant was lying in state, just as Lenin's had in 1924. The crowd kept growing, and since the two hills on either side of the square acted as a bottleneck, the pressure became unbearable. The two of us found it very difficult to breathe, let alone to move, but finally we managed to elbow our way out of the mob. I found out later that hundreds of people had been asphyxiated, and some police horses trampled to death. And so, I thought, even after he's dead Stalin goes on slaughtering the innocents.

Since my father was then still in prison, and I had been sacked from the mausoleum laboratory, the task of embalming Stalin's body fell to Mardashev and my former pupil Debov, who had recently been taken on to the staff of the lab. The corpse was brought to the laboratory only two hours after the official announcement of the General Secretary's death. Debov told me later of his surprise when he saw that Stalin's face looked very different from the image used for propaganda purposes, for it was

March 1953. Stalin's coffin in front of the mausoleum.

covered with pockmarks and liver spots, blemishes never seen by the public.

A new catafalque was installed beside the one that held Lenin's body, and the Cyrillic inscription on the front of the mausoleum was amended to read:

LENIN

STALIN

Eight years later, however, in 1961, Stalin's body was secretly removed from the mausoleum and, in accordance with a resolution of the Twenty-Second Party Congress, buried under the ramparts of the Kremlin among the graves of other dignitaries of the regime. The name "STALIN" disappeared from the mausoleum's façade. Khrushchev, who meanwhile had denounced the tyrant's crimes at the Twentieth Congress in January

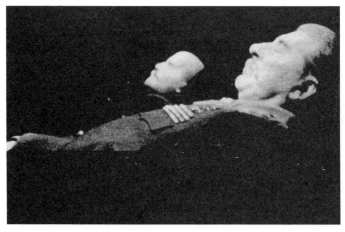

From 1953 to 1961, Stalin's body lay in the mausoleum beside that of Lenin. This photograph was taken secretly by an American journalist.

1956, is supposed to have said on that occasion, "The mausoleum stinks of Stalin's corpse." Quick to catch the new mood, the Muscovites invented the saying: "Don't sleep in a mausoleum that doesn't belong to you."

My father, however, did not live long enough to enjoy life under a regime other than Josef Stalin's. He had suffered frequent heart attacks during his time in prison, and these now started up again. On 7 October 1954, having had to break off in the middle of a lecture, he suffered a fatal seizure. The autopsy revealed an occlusion of the left coronary artery, the harsh conditions he had endured in gaol having probably accelerated his death. Of the twenty-one months during which he was behind bars in Boutyrki in Moscow, he spent eight in the prison hospital. He was by then suffering from atherocardiosclerosis, myocardio-dystrophy, and pulmonary emphysema, and was so weak he was declared unfit for any physical labour. I never found out whether he had been tortured. I avoided such subjects when talking to him: the KGB had installed such powerful microphones in the streets that they could pick up conversations between individuals in their own houses.

I learnt much later, while consulting the KGB archives in 1992, that no sentence had been pronounced against him. The preparation of the case for the trial lasted the twenty-one months of his imprisonment and was eventually stopped. I was also able to read the transcripts of the cross-examinations. The "judge" carrying out the preliminary investigations into his case began by reproaching him for his past as a Revolutionary Socialist. "You represented the RS at the Constituent Assembly . . . you fought against the Bolsheviks!" My father did not deny having been an RS deputy, but pointed out that after the dissolution of the Constituent Assembly he had ceased to have any connection with Revolutionary Socialists.

More serious was the charge that Rykov, Bukharin and Yagoda had been his friends. "What were your relations with Rykov, the most terrible enemy of the Party and the Soviet people?" asked the judge. "I did know him," my father replied, "but I never talked to him about politics." This was not altogether true. While we were staying at the dacha politics were sometimes discussed, often in terms highly critical of Stalin. That, however, was something my father could not have admitted: it would have cost him his life.

For all of that life, he had striven to present an image of himself as a Soviet citizen above all suspicion, with friends among the highest state officials. Now he saw those same friendships, and his zeal as an exemplary comrade, turned against him.

Nor did his tormentors leave matters there, for they also accused him of the supreme sin of "Jewish nationalism". They alleged, quite falsely, that he had had links with the Jewish Anti-Fascist Committee, and that after Mikhoels's death the committee had discussed replacing the latter with my father. "And who instructed you to embalm Mikhoels's body?" asked the judge, as though the embalming were indisputable proof that my father supported the Anti-Fascist Committee's activities.

More absurd still was the accusation that, in his book on the mausoleum, he had gone to the trouble of adding a goatee to a photograph of one of the guards of Lenin's coffin, making him look rather like Trotsky. No matter how much my father insisted that there was no such goatee in any of the copies of the book that he had seen himself, the judge would not listen. For him, this was just another indication of my father's involvement with the "rightist Trotskyite bloc".

Even in the months after Stalin's death my attempts to find work met with all kinds of humiliation. I applied to the Ministries of Health, Education and Food, but always without success. Then I heard that some of my colleagues who'd lost their jobs had managed to find employment in the provinces, so I decided to apply to the Ministry of Health again, saying that I was willing to work outside Moscow.

I was received by the Minister himself, a man called Stepanov. He said straight away that he had nothing for me. I asked him the reason for such a sweeping rejection. "You're not a doctor, are you?" he said rudely. I pointed out that Pasteur had not been a doctor either, but that had not stopped him from working in that field. "How dare you compare yourself to Pasteur!" he shouted, and drove me out of his office as though I were the scum of the earth.

Not long after my father was freed, a woman friend of my wife's who worked in the Ministry of Health told me, in the strictest secrecy, that it had been decided that I could go back to my job at the Institute of Oncology, but that to speed things up I needed to grease the palm of an official at the Ministry. We were so poor by now, however, that I could not find the necessary sum. I had to wait two long months before the assistant to the Director of the Institute bothered to telephone and invite me to take up my post again as head of the biochemistry lab.

Even so, my earnings there were not enough to keep a family of four, and I therefore kept on looking for work. In 1956, when the political situation was beginning to grow more relaxed, I began at last to receive some offers. The most promising came from Mardashev, by now head of the mausoleum laboratory: he asked me to join him as his assistant, and also to fill the place left vacant by my father's death as second professor in the biochemistry department at the Moscow First Medical Institute.

After thinking it over I decided to accept Mardashev's offer, little realizing that in doing so I was exposing myself to more humiliation. Maria Kovrigina, the new Minister of Health, opposed my appointment to the laboratory. The blind inertia of the Stalinist system was still so strong that, even three years after the dictator's death, there were still officials anxious to oppose my appointment simply because my father and I had fallen into disfavour under Stalin. There was to be further proof of this when, although I won a majority of the votes of the jury in a competitive examination held by the Institute of Biophysics, the head of radiobiological research at the Ministry of Health rejected my nomination. The post went to a candidate who hadn't won any votes at all.

I owed my eventual salvation to a friend, Georgi Smirnov, the Vice-Director of the Institute of Animal Morphology at the Academy of Sciences, who offered to create a biochemistry laboratory for me in his own institute. I accepted, and since my research was mainly concerned with nuclei and other parts of the cell, my new domain was christened "the laboratory for the biochemistry of cellular structures". My acceptance of this appointment, however, ended any hope I might have cherished of one day working again in the laboratory of the mausoleum, where the scientific resources were far greater.

XII

The Mausoleum Laboratory Goes International

"The embalmers' multinational"

In the late 1940s the range of the mausoleum laboratory's activities widened. It now undertook to preserve the bodies of heads of foreign Communist states, thus becoming a kind of world centre of embalming.

The internationalization of the laboratory's activities was largely due to the fact that after 1945 it enjoyed much better scientific facilities and material resources. The staff, too, was considerably enlarged. In 1939 it had employed only four scientists; after the war there were thirty-five. Our ranks were swelled by an army of histologists, anatomists, biochemists, physical chemists and opticians. It was at this time, too, that we increased our research into the composition of the skin and of subcutaneous cellular tissue, as well as into the autolytic factors affecting the decomposition of tissues.

Between 1949 and 1995 – that is, for nearly half a century – the methods that had been used since before the Second World War on the body of Lenin (and, for a time, Stalin) were applied to a number of other corpses: those of Georgi Dimitrov, leader of the

Bulgarian Communist Party; Horloogiyn Choybalsan, the Stalinist dictator of Mongolia; Klement Gottwald, leader of the Czech CP; Ho Chi Minh, President of North Vietnam; Agostinho Neto, leader of the People's Republic of Angola; Lindon Forbes Burnham, President of the Co-operative Republic of Guyana; and Kim Il Sung, the tyrant of North Korea.

Of all the embalmings carried out abroad, I myself took part only in those of Dimitrov and Choybalsan. My dismissal from the laboratory in 1952 excluded me from the rest.

On 2 July 1949 Georgi Dimitrov, head of the Bulgarian Communist Party and former leader of the Communist International, died in Moscow. His historical importance qualified him

The embalmed corpse of Georgi Dimitrov, head of the Bulgarian Communist Party and a former leader of the Communist International, who died in 1949. Scientists from the mausoleum travelled to Sofia to carry out the embalming. In 1990, however, Bulgarian democrats had the body removed and buried.

for embalming – or such at least was the opinion of the Bulgarian authorities, who considered that he had acquired legendary status through his courage at the Leipzig trial in 1933. Falsely accused by the Nazis of having been behind the burning of the Reichstag, he was released after demonstrating to the court that there was no proof against him and two of his Bulgarian "comrades". The Nazis, who were the real instigators of the fire, were thus thoroughly confounded.

A special train, similar to the one that had taken Lenin's body to Tiumen during the war, was hired to take Dimitrov's corpse back to Sofia, and my father and I went with it. That summer was swelteringly hot. The windows of the coach carrying the corpse had been sealed up with dark material, and the air inside was heavy with the scent of the countless wreaths piled round the coffin.

The passengers on the train included a Soviet government delegation headed by Marshal K.E. Voroshilov, a member of the Politburo and one of the people responsible for the complete unpreparedness of the Soviet armed forces at the beginning of the war with Germany. It seemed astonishing to me that such a man could still be treated as one of the highest dignitaries of the state.

Our train enjoyed special privileges. We were travelling without passports or diplomatic credentials, and we were not subjected to any checks on the Bulgarian border. I could not help thinking of the train on which, in 1917, Lenin and a handful of Bolsheviks were able, with financial and diplomatic help from Germany, to pass freely through all the frontiers of eastern Europe on their way to Petrograd (as St Petersburg was known from 1914 until Lenin's death in 1924, when it became Leningrad). Crossing the Danube at night we could see reflections of the lights of Ruse, a Bulgarian town on the south bank of the river, shimmering on the broad waters.

When we reached Sofia we were surprised to find Dimitrov's mausoleum ready, for he had not been dead more than a few days. This monument has been built in the capital main's square and, except that it was smaller and white in colour, was rather reminiscent of Lenin's mausoleum. Rectangular in shape, on top was a platform from which the Bulgarian leaders, like their comrades in Moscow, would review the parades that took place in Sofia on 7 November and 1 May each year, and on various national holidays.

After the funeral ceremony, representatives of Communist Parties from all over the world, including Maurice Thorez, General Secretary of the French CP, and Harry Pollitt, his British counterpart, were invited to a great banquet given by the Bulgarian government. Mardashev, my father and I were put up at the Vranya Palace, which before the war had belonged to King Boris III of Bulgaria. The old-fashioned "European" charm of the place delighted me, for it was full of caryatids, figures of Atlas bearing the world, gilded cupids, trompe-l'œil ceilings and fine furniture. Two Bulgarian secret service men were permanently at our disposal. They looked after us hand and foot, buying newspapers for us, taking our clothes to the cleaner, arranging for visits from the barber. I had never lived in such luxury.

The food at the banquet was delicious – game with a piquant sauce, smoked fish, blanquette de veau – and was accompanied by five different kinds of wine. However often we declined the endless succession of bottles, our hosts kept opening more. The explanation for this was that when we shook our heads the Bulgarians thought we meant "yes", the result of an oriental tradition they had inherited from the Turkish invader.[44]

Two rooms in the palace had been hastily converted into a laboratory where we could work on the corpse. The embalming of Dimitrov involved much the same procedure as that used for Lenin, except that the Bulgarian leader's corpse was in much better condition, and so our task was easier. For the first week my father and I worked on our own, fixing the tissues with formalin. The combination of the fumes of the formalin and the suffocating summer heat made us retch.

In my spare moments I wandered round the streets of Sofia, finding the cheerful atmosphere a great contrast to the monotony and gloom of life in Russia. The shops were well stocked with all kinds of goods; people wore brightly coloured clothes; the students sang and danced till late into the night. In short, Bulgaria had managed thus far to avoid becoming completely "socialist".

While we were in Sofia I talked to the handful of scientists who had known Vorobiov during his days there. They all had vivid memories of his lectures and of the lively parties he had given at his home or in restaurants. One professor told me he had some of Vorobiov's letters, and I, hoping to discover a new facet of the person I had been so fond of, asked him to let me see them. Mardashev, however, sternly advised me not to read them, on the grounds that they might prove to be compromising. Naturally, therefore, I had to forgo that pleasure.

When the main part of our work was completed, Mardashev and I were invited to go and spend ten days relaxing in the sanatorium at Euxinograd on the Black Sea, the resort where Party chiefs, ministers and diplomats from "sister States" used to spend their vacations together. We stayed in a palatial pink residence with light, spacious rooms and grounds sloping gently down to a white sandy beach. From the window of my room I could see a big pontoon on close-set piles designed to act as a breakwater for the "comrades" when they took a dip. Most of the guests spoke only very little Russian, and in any case conversation was very discreet. Everyone was afraid of saying something that might be misconstrued, so that our talk tended to be all of the weather, the healthy look of Bulgarian tomatoes and the deliciousness of the yoghurt.

One day – I remember we had been invited to go sailing – I made the acquaintance of an Albanian diplomat. The wife of the Soviet Ambassador in Sofia, who had been trying to listen in on our conversation, interrupted us to ask me what language we were speaking. "French," I told her. "Why French?" she asked. I explained that it was the only foreign language the Albanian understood. "Tell him to learn Russian, then, like everyone else!" she snapped. While I found this attitude appalling, it was typical at that time. Since the victory over Germany and the annexation of Eastern Europe, Greater Russian chauvinism had taken wings.

The embalming of Dimitrov was completed in less than three months, but before we went back to Moscow the Bulgarian leaders indicated that they wished to reward us handsomely for our labours. We rubbed our hands at the thought of being able to improve our wretched existences a little. Before any money could change hands, however, the Bulgarian government had to get permission from Moscow. We did not have to wait long for our own government's answer: "The embalming is a gift to Bulgaria from the USSR"!

Neither my father nor I ever set foot in Sofia again, although members of our staff did go there regularly to check the condition of Dimitrov's mummy. It remained in its mausoleum for forty years. Then, in July 1990, the Bulgarian democrats decided to take it away and bury it in a cemetery, close to the grave of Dimitrov's Protestant parents.

In February 1952 I went on my last foreign trip for the laboratory. My father was in bed at that time, recovering from a gall-bladder operation, and his assistant, Sergei Mardashev, had replaced him. Piotr Yegorov, chief physician at the Kremlin, rang me up and asked me to go as a matter of urgency to the mortuary of the Kremlin Hospital. Mardashev came with me.

We arrived to find the clothed body of a large man, clearly, from his eyes, an Oriental, lying on a long metal sink. No one dared tell us who it was. For a moment we thought it might be Mao Tse-tung, but as there was no sign of Poskrebychev, Stalin's secretary, who was always present on such momentous occasions, we ruled out that possibility.

Plain-clothes men from the Ministry of State Security were carefully searching the body. Next, the corpse was stripped and an anatomical pathologist carried out an autopsy, injecting formalin into the aorta, then examining the internal organs. When he announced the result, we heard one of those present heave a sigh of relief. This was the surgeon A.N. Bakulev, President of the Academy of Medical Sciences. A few hours earlier he had operated to remove a primary tumour from the body of the unknown, but then still living, man, and had been in a panic in case he should be held responsible for the patient's death. He was therefore greatly reassured to learn that the body was riddled with metastases. "God knows what would have become of me otherwise," he whispered to me.

We then learned we were to take the body away to some distant country and embalm it there. We were still told nothing about its identity. Only a few hours before we left were we informed that the corpse was that of the Mongolian dictator Marshal Horloogiyn Choybalsan, and that we were to accompany it to Ulan Bator.

After several days on the train we arrived, exhausted, in the Mongolian capital. Ulan Bator was only a small town really, with a few permanent houses, a university, a theatre, a hotel, and a government building. The latter included the mausoleum of Sukhe Bator, founder of the Socialist Republic of Mongolia, which was also to be the resting place of his successor, Choybalsan. The permanent buildings were the only visible signs of socialism. The rest of the town consisted of yurts – tents made of stretched hides – with camels and horses grazing among them.

It was from this nation of nomads that Choybalsan, formerly leader of a rebellious union of shepherds, had derived his power, power he had had no difficulty in retaining with financial and military aid from the USSR. Furthermore, although the Mongolian tyrant was now dead, Ulan Bator was still taking orders from Moscow. We had proof of this when we were granted an interview with Yumzhagiyen Tsedenbal, the new leader: he never ventured on an opinion without consulting the Soviet adviser who was always at his side.

It was also on orders from the Kremlin that Choybalsan's body was not to be accorded long-term preservation; Mongolia, with its population of a mere million or so, did not rate such a favour. Once we had completed the initial work of embalming, therefore, the dictator's remains were simply sealed up in the vault of his mausoleum. It was the end for me, too. I returned to Moscow to suffer, within only a few weeks, the arrest of my father and the loss of my own jobs. I was never to work for the mausoleum in Red Square again.

* *

On 14 March 1953, Klement Gottwald, head of the Czech Communist Party, died in Prague of the after-effects of the pneumonia he had contracted at Stalin's funeral. In a way, therefore, Gottwald too was a posthumous victim of the tyrant. His body was embalmed in Czechslovakia by scientists from the mausoleum, and remained in its own mausoleum in Prague until 1956, the year in which the post-Stalin "thaw" began in the Soviet Union and the Eastern Bloc; it was then cremated and the ashes placed in the Pantheon. "Embalming is not part of our national tradition," said the leaders of the Czech CP.

The year of the hundredth anniversary of Lenin's birth, 1970, marked an important turning point in the history of the mausoleum laboratory. The Politburo agreed to the purchase

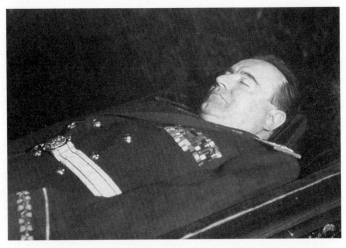

The embalmed corpse of Klement Gottwald, head of the Czech Communist Party, who died in 1953. The body was on display in Prague for three years, before being removed and cremated in 1956, the year in which the post-Stalin "thaw" began.

of a good deal of modern equipment from abroad: centrifuges, electronic microscopes, automatic analysers of amino-acid compounds, spectrophotometers, and so on, together worth several million dollars. Fifty more scientists were recruited to the staff, making almost a hundred in all. Lenin's corpse could now be photographed with special cameras, analysed in the minutest detail and, where necessary, repaired or restored. The procedure worked out by Vorobiov and my father was considerably improved on, becoming so effective that even if it were eventually decided that a body should be buried, it would still appear quite lifelike after months or even years.

Every scientist on the staff of the lab had a corpse at his disposal on which to carry out his own experiments; he was kept completely ignorant of its identity. Even today there is still a kind of "secret museum" of such nameless bodies in the laboratory. Most are kept under glass covers, but some have been forgotten for years and lie in their "balsam" baths, their hair floating like seaweed. It is a sight that can have few parallels anywhere in the world.

In 1969 the staff of the mausoleum laboratory were entrusted with another foreign mission: the embalming of Ho Chi Minh, leader of the Viet Minh against the French and then of the North Vietnamese in the war against South Vietnam and the United States. This episode, one of the best-kept secrets in the history of the mausoleum, was described to me by a scientist who still works in the laboratory. This is what he told me:

"The first time I went to North Vietnam was in October 1971. I can still remember the day I got there. As our plane flew over the region near Hanoi, the earth below was burning. The American air force had been bombing the city more and more heavily for several weeks. Then the Phantoms[45] escorting our plane from Laos to Vietnam turned back. A few seconds later the air corridor under American protection ended.

"We landed at Zalam airport on the banks of the Red River. It was unbearably hot: forty degrees, with nearly one hundred per cent humidity even though it was autumn. We were met by a small delegation of North Vietnamese officers, who all asked after my health and that of my wife and children. 'Oriental courtesy', I thought as I listened to their endless urbanities. I was offered a minute cup into which someone poured a bitter yellow liquid. Green tea. I'd never tasted it before.

"On the way in to Hanoi I noticed a huge steel structure nearly a kilometre and a half long. "That's Lambigne Bridge, the biggest in the Far East", one of my hosts told me. "It was built nearly a hundred years ago by the French engineer Gustave Eiffel – the one who built the Eiffel Tower." I was astonished to see this august structure standing after being subjected to so much bombing.

"In Hanoi I was put up in a fine colonial-style house that had belonged to a French general before the war.[46] My visit was often interrupted by the loud whine of air-raid sirens. The streets would empty in the twinkling of an eye. Everyone took shelter wherever they could – in cellars, sewers or under the bridges.

"After three days I was taken through the jungle to a place near Chantai, a small town about thirty kilometres from the capital. Soldiers armed with machetes were hacking out a track called the 'Path of the Cockerel'. Nestling among the trees was a building of light-brown brick: the tomb of Ho Chi Minh. It was a faithful replica of Lenin's mausoleum, though smaller – only 60 square metres. It looked like a toy.

"I was taken inside, where I found air-conditioning apparatus, a

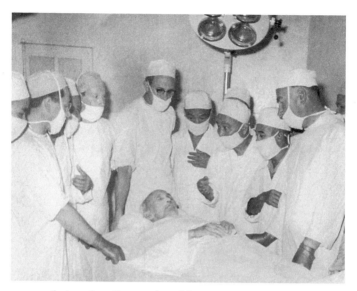

1971 – the team from the mausoleum laboratory with Vietnamese scientists beside the body of Ho Chi Minh, President of North Vietnam until his death in 1969. Most of the work was carried out at a secret laboratory in the jungle, largely for fear of American bombing.

bath, and jars of chemicals – in short, all the equipment required for embalming the body. I was amazed at the ingenuity of the Vietnamese, who had managed to bring running water, electricity and telephone lines secretly through the jungle. Underneath the mausoleum was a corridor ten metres deep leading to a concrete chamber to which the body was removed during air raids. Beneath his glass cover Ho Chi Minh, with his little beard and white suit, looked like a wealthy Chinese mandarin.

"A long brick passage, its roof covered with branches as camouflage against American reconnaissance planes, took us from the mausoleum to a large terrace under which was a house – a permanent structure, not a tent – in which my colleagues Sergei Debov and Yuri Denissov-Nikolsky were staying.

"Since the death of Ho Chi Minh in September 1969 the Soviet authorities had spared no effort to help the North Vietnamese embalm the body of their historic leader. A team of scientists from the laboratory of the Lenin mausoleum had been specially sent by air from Moscow. The work of preservation was originally to have been done in a laboratory in the grounds of a military hospital near the Pasteur Institute in Hanoi. But when the air raids on the capital intensified the laboratory was moved to the Chantai area.

"In spring 1971 an unexpected incident had taken place about a kilometre and a half from the mausoleum. While the officer in charge of the secret base was having tea in the forest with the deputy head of the North Vietnamese Army's anti-aircraft defences, an American helicopter flew overhead only a few yards away. It was following the course of the Red River, with its cabin door wide open and some Yankee paratroopers keeping cool by dangling their legs through the aperture.

"Some other US helicopters flew over the river, too, then landed on the opposite bank. The Americans were looking for some of their compatriots who had been kept in a camp near by. But the place had been deserted long since, and the paras had to go away empty-handed.

"Though the Americans hadn't noticed the presence of enemy troops in the area, the episode was enough to make the North Vietnamese generals decide to strengthen the security around the mausoleum. Ho's body was regarded as sacred, and they knew that its capture or destruction would deal a fatal blow to the morale of their troops. 'If the Yankees ever did get hold of it,' a general on the base told us one day, 'we'd be prepared to hand over all our American prisoners in exchange for it.' The American intelligence services, well aware of this, had stepped up their search.

"At the time I started working at the base it was guarded by no fewer than a hundred soldiers and equipped with powerful anti-aircraft guns. The house we lived in was protected by three tanks. Every morning we could see the gunners polishing shells – we were always afraid they might drop one by mistake. Debov even woke up one morning to find a tank's gun trained on his window. We had a good laugh about that.

"But we were still pretty anxious. There was a big hill about a hundred metres from the base which the American planes used as a bearing for flying over Hanoi. The noise of their jet engines was deafening, and we were always afraid they might spot us.

"One day we had a visit from a colleague who had spent some time in the capital. 'At least it's nice and peaceful here,' he said. 'Not like in Hanoi, where we're always being disturbed by air raids.' Then, just as he was raising a spoonful of soup to his lips, the air-raid warning sounded. He put down his spoon, then, after a long silence, tried again. But the siren went off again. He made four attempts, but never finished his lunch. By the time he got back to it his soup was cold.

"In April 1972 there was another escalation in the hostilities. The sound of the bombing came nearer and nearer, so it was decided that the body should be moved somewhere safer. The precious object was put on board an amphibious craft and floated some fifteen kilometres down the Red River. Then the vehicle landed and a brigade of soldiers dug and hacked a way for it through the vegetation, while, in the rear, other troops obliterated all tell-tale traces of their passage with demolition charges.

"The body was transported to an enormous cave. I was told there are a number of these vast natural grottoes in Vietnam, some of which have been converted into cathedrals. Inside, ours was as high as a ten-storey building, and equipped in the same way as the jungle mausoleum with running water, electricity, air conditioning, a laboratory, and accommodation for the scientists and guards.

"In December 1972, just after the worst phase of the bombing, the body was taken back to its temporary mausoleum. Meanwhile in Hanoi work had been going on in secret that would soon result in the largest mausoleum in the world. It was a kind of gigantic Roman temple, and was finished just after the signing of the peace. It's the tallest building in the capital, designed to be visible from the country miles around.

"The sarcophagus lies in a huge white chamber at the top of the monument. So powerful is the air-conditioning system that condensation always seem to be running down the walls, because of the difference between the inside temperature, kept at sixteen degrees, and the outside temperature of about forty degrees. Below is the leaders' viewing platform. Behind the building there is now a sweet-smelling garden of tropical flowers and dwarf trees."

Twenty-seven years after his death, the revolutionary of the Viet Minh and of North Vietnam still reposes in his mausoleum in Badigne Square. Russian scientists continue to pay regular visits to his corpse.

In 1979 there was another embalming, this time of Dr Agostinho Neto, the President of the People's Republic of Angola. Here the mausoleum's experts who travelled to the capital, Luanda, to carry out their work, had to deal with the particular

*The embalmed corpse of Agostinho Neto, President of Angola,
who died in 1979.*

problems associated with black skin. After experimenting for
three months the Russian scientists found that the addition of
lipid antioxidant preserved the natural colour of the skin. With
that resolved, however, there followed a bizarre argument. Some
Angolan leaders wanted Neto, who had been a doctor before he
became a revolutionary, to wear spectacles. Others objected, on
the grounds that the effect of reflection from the lenses on the
dark skin would be disfiguring. In the end a compromise was
reached: Neto would wear glasses that had no lenses.

To make matters even more difficult, the embalming was
carried out against a background of civil war. Opponents of
the "People's Republic of Angola" cut the cable supplying power
to the air-conditioning system. The outside temperature was
so high there was a danger the corpse would decompose. An

enterprising Angolan commissar then had the bright idea of requisitioning ice from the local ice-cream factory, and the corpse was saved *in extremis*.

Initially Agostinho Neto's mausoleum in Luanda was intended to be a huge tower visible from the sea, and was to be built by Soviet workmen in less than a year. The necessary stone and marble were stolen from neighbouring villas, but because of inadequate funding the work was never completed. The body, however, lay in state on one day a year – the "Day of the Hero" – although Neto's widow, a famous Portuguese poetess, was allowed to go and visit her husband's embalmed corpse whenever she wished. Thirteen years later, however, in December 1992, the Angolan government finally decided, in accordance with his widow's wishes, to bury him.

Next came Lindon Forbes Burnham, President of the Co-operative Republic of Guyana, who was embalmed in 1985. Guyana was difficult to get to – there was no direct flight between Moscow and Georgetown – so the mausoleum's scientists did not arrive until two weeks after the death, by which time the corpse was showing signs of advanced decomposition. The Soviet experts' task was already complicated by the fact that certain patches on the face were lacking in pigmentation, the result of skin disease. Because of these technical problems the embalming procedure, which was carried out in Moscow, took more than nine months. The body was then flown back to Georgetown, where on the first anniversary of Burnham's death it was supposed to be installed, housed in a plexiglass capsule, in the centre of a cross-shaped mausoleum designed by an American architect.

But the US State Department decided otherwise. Since Burnham's death Angola had undergone a change of political regime, and the United States was now threatening to cut off economic aid if the Guyanese authorities insisted on their late leader's body lying in state. The US government could not tolerate the idea that a rite initiated and perfected by the USSR should be observed in Latin America, which America regarded as her own preserve. After a sumptuous funeral, therefore, Burnham's body was walled up in the pedestal of the sarcophagus. I do not know what condition it is in now, although the plexiglass container will probably have helped it withstand the ravages of time.

Thus the bodies of those Communist heads of state deemed worthy of such treatment were all embalmed by Soviet scientists. The only exception was Mao Tse-tung, the "Great Helmsman", whose remains Chinese experts managed to preserve themselves. Western newspapers report every so often that Mao's body is in an advanced state of putrefaction. It should be remembered, however, that before the 1949 revolution China already had a long tradition of embalming her emperors and other dignitaries.

It may be worth making a few general remarks here about the internationalization of embalming that began after the war.

The long-term preservation of the body of a head of state was always carried out at the request of the national government concerned, and never at the behest of Moscow.

The leaders of "sister states" who had recourse to the services of the laboratory of the mausoleum in Moscow usually had two objects in view: to reinforce the legitimacy of their regime by preserving the body of their "historic" leader, and to ingratiate themselves with their big brother, the USSR. It should also be noted that every one of the leaders who have been embalmed was a dictator who, when he was alive, had already allowed a personality cult to develop around his life, character and works.

The only example of embalming carried out in a country with a wholly Western culture is that of Klement Gottwald, though it may be remembered that his body was cremated in 1956, despite the risk to the Czechs of offending the authorities in Moscow. I might be tempted, therefore, to conclude that embalming is not compatible with the traditions of civilized countries. If I were to say that, however, I run the risk of incurring the wrath of my colleagues in the laboratory of the mausoleum. Moreover, there can be no doubt that their work remains of considerable scientific value.

XIII

Embalmers of the Nouveaux Riches

I am now eighty-four years old. For four-fifths of my life I suffered, like most of my fellow citizens, under the inhuman political regimes imposed by Stalin and his successors. During all those years I have always kept in mind the Party's lies about "the radiant future of Communism"; kept in mind, too, the arrests, the show trials, the mass executions.

More than ten years have gone by since the process of democratization started by Mikhail Gorbachev began. In Russia, freedom of the individual, of the press and of religion have become reality. I, as much or more than anyone, relish the possibility now given to us of living without fear of being arrested injustly, and of travelling freely all over the world – provided, of course, that one can afford it.

For that is the other side of the coin as far as the "new Russia" is concerned. Instead of the Berlin Wall separating East from West both symbolically and physically, we now have the wall of money. Since the introduction in January 1992 of liberal reforms that have resulted in hyper-inflation and a precipitous fall of the rouble against the dollar, our people have become a great deal poorer. To take science alone, state funding has been reduced by 95 per cent since 1991. Our scientists, who once held distinguished positions

Professor Zbarsky at home during his research into the photographic archives of the Lenin mausoleum.

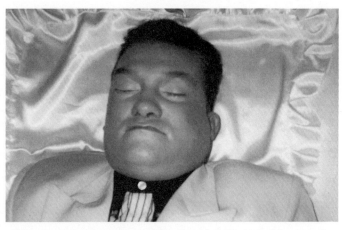

The body of a Russian nouveau riche after embalming in the laboratory that preserves Lenin's body. This new style of embalming is not intended to last several decades, as was planned from the start for Lenin; instead, bodies are only prepared for the funeral. Even so, the liquid used is so efficient that once buried, corpses stay in good condition for months.

in society and had salaries to match, now earn less than the equivalent of 100 dollars a month, and are obliged to engage in business activities in order to stay alive. The youngest and the most gifted go abroad. Those who remain are losing faith in science, partly because of the lack of adequate resources and equipment.

It is the same story with the laboratory of the mausoleum. Before 1991 the state contributed 100 per cent of its budget; now it gives only 20 per cent. As a result the lab found itself looking for other ways of ensuring its survival. At that point Yuri Lujkov, the Mayor of Moscow, worried about the deplorable state of the funeral provisions inherited from the Communist regime, had the bright idea of letting the staff of the mausoleum set up Ritual Service, a company that handles embalmings at the mausoleum lab for the nouveaux riches.

This proved to be very timely. The crime rate was shooting up – nearly twenty-five thousand murders had been committed in Russia during the previous year. Since many of these nouveaux riches were gangsters of one kind or another, and since gang warfare had become endemic, orders soon started to come in at an average rate of four embalmings a month. I am indebted to a scientist who now works in the mausoleum lab for a description of how this kind of embalming is carried out.

To begin with, the commercial director of Ritual Service meets the family of the murdered nouveau riche, and between them they draw up a list of what is to be done: restoration of colour to the skin of the hands and face; restoration of flexibility to the arms and neck, and so on. A number from one to six is written down beside each heading on the list, according to how the family responds to each suggestion. Using these figures, it is possible, apparently, to arrive at a fairly accurate idea of the client's resources. Charges range from 1,500 US dollars for a single day's work (for example, when the head has not been smashed to a pulp by bullets) to 10,000 US dollars for a whole week (if the whole body was blown to pieces by a bomb and has to be put together again).

Once these details are agreed, the embalmers go to fetch the body from the mortuary. I was told that on one occasion a Russian mafioso knelt beside the corpse of a murdered friend and licked his wounds to show how much he had loved the dead man. At this edifying spectacle a young woman who worked in the mortuary, though used to the sight of corpses, fainted away.

The body of the nouveau riche is then taken to the mausoleum lab and laid on a table of thick grey marble – in fact, the one that was used for embalming Stalin. The scientists, who are not supposed to know the identity of the dead person, inject 8 litres of "balsam" into the arteries, helping it to circulate by massaging the arms and legs. In just a few seconds the hands turn from blue to ivory white. If the face has been badly damaged it is reconstructed with the aid of photographs, using pieces of bone and skin taken from other parts of the body. Then another scientist, the "beautician", goes to work with a box of makeup. Using foundation and lipstick, it is her job to restore the dead man's youth, and she must also ensure that any marks resulting from the murder disappear. Finally, a thin white tissue is placed on the forehead, since that is where the friends and relations will deposit a parting kiss.

I ought to add that this kind of embalming bears little resemblance to the method used for the long-term preservation of a body. Quite apart from anything else, the corpse is not immersed in a special bath, as was the case with Lenin. It is merely

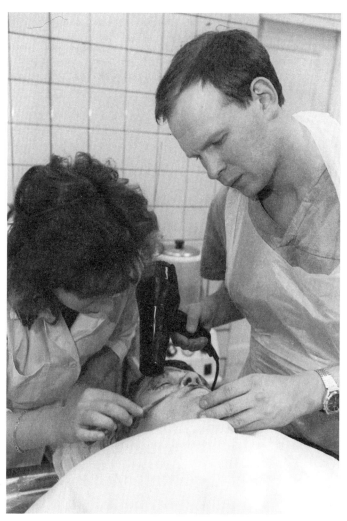

Two beauticians apply foundation cream to a gangster's face, after skin has been removed from one of his legs and sewn on to his cheek to hide a bullet wound.

"reconditioned" for the day of the funeral. On one occasion, however, Ritual Service did decide to check up on the efficiency of the preserving liquid it used, and exhumed one of its "clients" nine months after he had been embalmed. The body, it seems, was still in the same state as it had been just after the work had been completed.

Ritual Service also sells luxury coffins to the families of the nouveaux riches. Prices are steep, ranging from 5,000 dollars for a wooden coffin "Made in the USA" to 20,000 dollars for a crystal version made in Russia. The most popular model is the "Al Capone", an elaborate affair which got its name after someone saw a similar coffin in a video of *The Godfather*.

In fact, prices paid for embalming and a luxury coffin form only a relatively small part of the total bill for burying a gangster who has been gunned down. Before going into more detail about the burial rites of the Russian mafia, I should point out that they are particularly elaborate in Yekaterinburg (Sverdlovsk) in the eastern Urals, the capital of the heavily industrialized Oblast district.[47] I have therefore taken events in Yekaterinburg as a benchmark for these rites among Russia's nouveau-riche gangsters today.

For nearly six years this town has been the setting of bloody mafia war. Two gangs – "Centralny" ("Town Centre") and "Uralmash", named after the metallurgical complex, the largest in the country, located in the northern suburbs of the town – are engaged in a fight to the death for control of the business in the region and of the clandestine export of metals and precious stones from the mineral-rich Ural Mountains. All this is worth several million dollars a year, and is correspondingly dangerous. A local official involved in the fight against organized crime once told me that, taking only the leaders into account, Centralny has lost five of its bosses in this struggle for power, and Uralmash seven.

Nor is this war a simple matter of the settling of scores between local "families". The gangs' activities affect all of Russia, and even other countries. For example, Uralmash "protects" the market for the import of cars into Vladivostock, as well as freight in and out of Moscow International Airport; it also controls banks whose interests stretch as far as the London metals market. Backed by a unified financial system and a thousand active members in the Urals region alone, Uralmash, according to the Moscow police, is the most powerful gang in Russia.

Moreover, when one of them loses a godfather, both Uralmash and Centralny give him a send-off worthy of a head of state. I have been told that of all the funerals that ever took place in Yekaterinburg, that of Oleg Vagin, the godfather of Centralny, was by far the most sumptuous. The day after he was murdered his remains and those of his three bodyguards who died with him lay in state in the middle of the casino he ran. The four coffins were then carried by pallbearers along a route that ran for three kilometres through the town. Ten police cars closed the town centre to traffic so that the procession could pass through – in theory, a privilege that belongs only to the highest government dignitaries.

After the funeral mass, which was celebrated by the city's most fashionable archimandrite, representatives of every clan were supposed to kiss the corpse. There is no escaping this ritual, for any abstention is at once interpreted as an avowal of guilt. In the case of Oleg Vagin's murder, all Centralny's men were sure Uralmash was responsible. Their suspicions were strengthened by the absence from the church of Constantin Tziganovm, the godfather of Uralmash. Eventually he showed up at the cemetery surrounded by about ten bodyguards. Nevertheless, and despite the looks of loathing he had to endure, he managed to kiss Vagin on the face just before he was buried.

On these occasions, while the clods of earth are raining down on the coffin, friends and relations of the deceased throw banknotes into the grave so that he will not be without means in the afterlife. All those present are then invited to a funeral banquet. Several thousand places were set for Vagin's burial feast, at which delicious food and fine wine were served. Everyone in the town suddenly turned out to have been a friend of Vagin's.

Once our mafioso is six feet underground, his family or friends hold a collection to pay for his tomb. In a cemetery in the north of Yekaterinburg, Uralmash's men have had erected an impressive

An assistant in a monumental mason's workshop in Yekaterinburg lays out a giant photograph of Vladimir Juldibin, a twenty-seven-year-old gangster murdered by a rival gang in 1995. The photographic image will be incorporated into the tombstone.

Workers in the cemetery at Uralmash erecting the giant tombstone
(nearly three metres high and costing 12,000 dollars) over the grave
of Vladimir Juldibin. The man who ordered it (in dark clothes)
supervises the work. He seems to be reflected in the tombstone
of his brother in arms, who was shot to death.

forest of black steles. The dead mafiosi are depicted in full-length, life-size photographic portraits engraved on to their gravestones, frozen for eternity in everyday situations. Dressed in their Adidas tracksuits, the regular uniform of Russian mafiosi, and leather jackets, holding caps or overnight bags in their hands, they seem to look on with a mocking air. It is true, too, that these tombstones, which cost the equivalent of at least 8,000 dollars, are beyond most people's purses, especially given that the average Russian salary is equal to about 125 dollars a month.

In another Yekaterinburg cemetery Mikhail Kuchin, a Centralny godfather, is represented on his tombstone in a

The graves of members of the "Uralmash" gang, considered to be the most powerful in Russia. The murderous war between two groups involved in organized crime in Yekaterinburg has caused the deaths of several of their leaders. In the last five years Uralmash is said to have lost seven of its bosses as against five in the case of "Centralny" ("Town Centre"), the other powerful gang in the town. What is at stake in this bloody settling of scores is the control of business in the heavily industrialized region, and of the market in metals and precious stones from the Ural Mountains, the whole worth several million dollars a year.

Tombstone (nearly three metres high) of local gangster Mikhail Kuchin in the cemetery at Uralmash, a working-class district in the northern suburbs of Yekaterinburg. The tombstone, made of semi-precious stones, cost 64,000 dollars. The image on the stone shows the gangster holding in his left hand the keys to his Mercedes, symbol of power in the new Russia.

double-breasted suit with wide lapels, crew-cut hair, and holding the keys of his Mercedes. The tomb itself, made of malachite and *zmeevick* (semi-precious stones from the Ural Mountains) is said to have cost his family and friends the trifling sum of 64,000 dollars. The record-holder for costly funerary monuments, however, is not a gangster, but Vagit Alekperov, the current executive president of Lukoil, Russia's largest oil company. Although very much still alive, he has not baulked at spending a quarter of a million dollars on a malachite mausoleum resembling a miniature Taj Mahal.

Finally, to return to murdered gangsters, on every anniversary of the dead man's birthday and the day of his death, his relatives and friends stage a feast among the tombs. On one occasion the family of Mikhail Kuchin, he of the Mercedes car keys, outdid all other contenders with an al fresco meal of stunning extravagance. On a green marble table close to her late husband's grave, Nadezhda Kuchina set out a luxurious array of tropical fruit, sturgeon, caviare, roast suckling pigs, petits fours, and giant bottles of vodka. These were the remains of a 10,000-dollar banquet given the evening before for Centralny's finest. After laying magnificent bouquets of flowers on the grave, the guests stuffed themselves and drank to the health of the departed. "The reason I wanted to make the grave so handsome," Nadezhda Kuchina once remarked, "is to make the people who ordered my husband's death go green with envy."

The recent extension of the mausoleum laboratory's activities to cover the embalming of mafiosi strikes me as typical of the depth to which the authority of the government of Russia has sunk in the last few years. For now it is no longer political leaders who have themselves embalmed, but the masters of the economy.

*Members of one of the Yekaterinburg gangs paying their respects at the
grave of one of their members. Most are under thirty-five years of age, and
have left their BMWs, Mercedeses and Cherokees parked outside the cemetery.
Such gatherings are usually held twice a year round the grave of a dead
comrade – on his birthday, and on the anniversary of his death.*

Taking advantage of the sudden change to a market economy, young men – their average age is no more than about thirty-five – have acquired, mainly through violence, control of large sectors of commerce and industry. When, in their turn, they become victims of the brutal society they themselves have helped to create, they die surrounded by wealth, a good deal of which they have often lavished on their family and friends. Small wonder then, that the latter are profoundly grateful, and wish to give their benefactors funerals fit for kings.

These flamboyant funeral rites also have a practical purpose, however. By putting up expensive memorials, the mafia families seek to challenge and defy the enemy (a rival gang, the police, or public opinion); to demonstrate that the loss of one of their leaders, painful though it may be, strengthens rather than weakens the power of the clan.

It seems, therefore, that no matter what the political regime, embalming and the building of mausoleums is, in twentieth-century Russia, both a homage paid to the dead and a demonstration of power addressed to the living. Thus, in the view of Stalin and his allies, the preservation of Lenin's body and the erection of the mausoleum in Red Square would not only signal Lenin's unique place in history; they would also symbolize a whole system of ideas that were destined to survive him and to become the basis of Soviet political life.

The embalming of Kim Il Sung, the Communist dictator of North Korea, in 1995 is, however, an exception in the recent development of the laboratory's activities, not least because the operation was largely instrumental in saving the laboratory from certain bankruptcy. The pittance paid to it by the mysterious "social aid fund" controlled by the new Communist Party of the

Russian Federation would certainly not have been enough to ensure the survival of such a costly mechanism. Nevertheless, such aid as the fund does provide is proof of the great attachment Russian Communists still feel for the body of their spiritual guide.

Admittedly, since 1992, voices have been raised in the democrats' camp, asking for Lenin to be buried. Anatoli Sobchak, a former Mayor of St Petersburg, has even suggested burying him beside his mother's grave in the Volkov cemetery. As we have seen, some historians have maintained that Nadezhda Krupskaya, Lenin's wife, was against the embalming in the first place, although the Communists retort that there are no written documents to back up these arguments. Nor could the Orthodox Church help putting in its pennyworth. Alexis II, the Patriarch of Moscow, went so far as to say that if Lenin was not buried, "his malign soul would go on hovering over the country, to its great detriment".

On 6 October 1993, two days after the attempted putsch by the Communists and nationalists had been put down, President Boris Yeltsin suddenly decided to abolish the mausoleum guard. At once rumours began to circulate to the effect that Lenin was about to be buried, and the Kremlin responded with an announcement that a decision would be made within the next six months. (In fact, such a decision was not made, nor has one been made since.) At this point the gutter press in Russia and in the West took advantage of the uncertainty to declare that the body was not authentic. The tabloid weekly *Argumenty i Fakty* ("Arguments and Facts") produced a piece of pure invention: "During its transfer to Tiumen in early July," it ran, "Lenin's body became covered with patches of mould. An unqualified assistant poured boiling water over them in the hope of getting rid of them. His colleagues quickly cleaned the body up, but after a quarter of an hour it was covered with blisters, and then it swiftly decomposed. Only the hands and face could be salvaged."[48]

Since I was a member of the team responsible for preserving Lenin's remains from 1934 to 1952, I view this sort of nonsense with indignation. I am now the last survivor of the team, and I consider it my duty towards my colleagues to say that – until 1952, at least – the corpse was preserved in excellent condition, and that it never entered our heads to "scald the body in order to clean it up." Nor was it our habit to leave the scientific surveillance of the corpse to an "unqualified assistant". I particularly regret that the author of the article did not take the trouble to consult me, especially as his "information" was repeated blindly by some quite respectable Western newspapers.

In March 1997, Yeltsin announced that a referendum would be held "in the near future" to decide what was to be done with the body in the mausoleum. He himself, he said, was in favour of burying Lenin beside his mother in St Petersburg, "according to his own express wish". This naturally provoked a general outcry in the Duma, the lower house of the Russian Parliament, where the Communist deputies hold the majority. They quickly passed a law forbidding any modification, however small, to Red Square. In support of their argument they invoked the fact that UNESCO had classified the Lenin mausoleum as a part of the "world's heritage".

This division among the leaders is reflected in public opinion. A poll published last spring showed that 48 per cent of Russians were in favour of burial, 38 per cent against, and the rest of those interviewed without an opinion. The debate will go on poisoning Russian political life for some time to come. Furthermore, it probably will not be until the generation of older Communists has died out that a decision will finally be made in favour of burial.

* *

From the eighteen years I spent at the mausoleum I drew two conclusions.

Throughout our time there, my father and I were physically so close to the source of power that we might easily have been swept away in the maelstrom of Stalin's purges. We probably owed our survival to the lack of people familiar with the techniques of preservation, for before the last war there were no more than four people really skilled in those procedures. Thus when Vorobiov died in 1937 there were only three of us left, so that to have eliminated even one of us would have been to put Lenin's corpse, the symbolic centre of Soviet power, in danger. When my father was arrested and I lost my job in 1952, we suddenly realized we were not safe any more. By then, the laboratory had expanded considerably, and had a far larger staff. We were no longer "irreplaceable". Even so, that we escaped death during one of the most dangerous periods of modern history was, ironically, due to the man who founded the state that might otherwise have "purged" us.

My second reflection is that while the preservation of Lenin's corpse was a considerable scientific achievement, I cannot help believing that embalming is a barbaric and anachronistic practice, alien to the cultures of Western societies. That is why, despite the privileges I enjoyed during the years I spent in the shadow and the shelter of the mausoleum – generous salary, modern equipment and scarce materials to work with, as well as access to a wealth of scientific literature – I believe, speaking as a citizen, that Lenin should now be buried.

10 July 1997
Moscow

*The stream of visitors to the mausoleum in the 1960s. Altogether, many,
many millions (about 14 million even before the Second World War)
of Russians and foreign visitors have visited this shrine to the
founder of Soviet Russia since its inauguration.*

Notes

1. B.V. Petrovsky, "V.I. Lenin's wound and illness", *Vestnik AN SSSR*, 1991, no.2, pp.114–30 (in Russian).

2. Hélène Carrère-d'Encausse, *Lénine, la révolution et le pouvoir* ("Lenin, Revolution and Power"), Paris, Flammarion, 1979.

3. This actually consisted of notes dictated on 23 and 31 December, to which was attached the addendum of 4 January 1923 mentioned in the following paragraph.

4. V.P. Ossipov, *Ogoniok*, 1990, no.4, pp.4–8.

5. N.V. Valentinov-Volsky, *The NEP and the Crisis in the Party after Lenin's Death*, California, Hoover Institution Press, Stanford University, 1971, pp.90–93.

6. OGPU (Russian initials for United State Political Administration) succeeded the GPU in 1923, which in turn had replaced the Cheka (properly, VeCheka, Russian acronym for All-Russian Extraordinary Commission for Combating Counter-Revolution and Sabotage), the first Soviet political police agency, established in December 1917. OGPU was in turn succeeded by the NKVD (People's Commissariat of Internal Affairs), 1934; NKGB (People's Commissariat of State Security), 1943; MGB (Ministry of State Security), 1946; MVD (Ministry of Internal Affairs), 1953. After Stalin's death in 1953, the political police was reorganized yet again, becoming the KGB (Commissariat of State Security) in 1954. With the break-up of the Soviet Union the KGB was itself divided and reorganized, some of its role being taken up by the newly formed FSB (Federal Security Service).

7. Russian Centre for the Preservation and Study of Contemporary Historical Documents (CRCEDHC), collection 16, inv.2s, un.con.42, f.90–93.

8. *Pravda*, 29 January 1924.

9. CRCEDHC, coll.16, inv.2s, un.con.49, f.4

10. *Izvestiya*, 26 January 1924.

11. CRCEDHC, coll.16, inv.2s, un.con.45, ff.1–2.

12. CRCEDHC, coll.16, inv.2s, un.con.47, ff.1–3 and 5.

13. CRCEDHC, coll.16, inv.2s, un.con.51, f.2.

14. *Kommunist* (Kharkov), 26 January 1924.

15. CRCEDHC, coll.16, inv.2s, un.con.54, f.2.

16. Y. Lopukhin, *Lenin's Illness, Death and Embalming*, Moscow, Respublica, 1997 (in Russian).

17. Autolysis – the process by which an organism's cells and tissues are destroyed by enzymes produced by the cells themselves.

18. CRCEDHC, coll. 16, inv.2s, un.con.52, ff.103–121.

19. CRCEDHC, coll.16, inv.2s, un.con.51, f.14 and un.con.52, ff.122–40.

20. CRCEDHC, coll.16, inv.2s, un.con.54, f.3.

21. CRCEDHC, coll.16, inv.2s, un.con.54, ff.6, 9.

22. CRCEDHC, coll.16, inv.2s, un.con.52, f. 51.

23. CRCEDHC, coll.16, inv.2s, un.con.51. f.16; *Pravda*, 25 March 1924.

24. Trotsky lost the power struggle with Stalin; in 1927 he was expelled from the Politburo, and two years later exiled from Russia. Eventually finding sanctuary in Mexico, he was assassinated there, almost certainly on Stalin's orders, in 1940. Declared a "non-person" by Stalin, his works were banned, he was "written out" of Soviet histories, and his name

and image were expunged from records and from anything that commemorated his work; even the mention of his name could bring severe punishment upon anyone who uttered it. He was officially taken off the list of non-persons in 1987, but has yet to be fully rehabilitated in Russia.

25. The largest church in Russia, destroyed by Stalin. The construction of a replica south-west of the Kremlin began in 1995.

26. George Gamov (1904–68) left the USSR in 1933 and achieved a distinguished career, especially as an astrophysicist in the United States (where he was known as Gamow).

27. Konsomol is an acronym of the Russian words for Communist Union of Youth. The organization was open to those aged between fourteen and twenty-six.

28. *Subotu* means Saturday in Russian, but as under the Communist regime that day was an ordinary working day, Sunday, the day for unpaid voluntary work, was called *subotnik*.

29. Formalin is a solution of the gas formaldehyde and water.

30. B.I. Zbarsky, *The Lenin Mausoleum*, Moscow, Gospolitizdat, 1944, pp.41–42 (in Russian).

31. Lenin had been born Vladimir Ilich Ulyanov, and began to use the pseudonym in about 1900. His elder brother, Alexander, was executed in 1887 for his part in an attempt on the life of Tsar Nicholas III.

32. B.I. Zbarsky, *The Lenin Mausoleum*, op.cit., p.50.

33. Nikitin's thwarted act of vandalism was the first of a long series of attacks upon Lenin's corpse. The records of the Kremlin Guard, whose duties include surveillance of the mausoleum, mention seven in all:

20 March 1959. A man threw a steel-handled hammer and broke the glass over the sarcophagus. The man's name is unknown, as is what happened to him afterwards. I remember my father telling me of a similar incident in 1939. Perhaps the two episodes were one and the same; perhaps not.

14 July 1960. A man called K. Mikhailov jumped over the safety barrier round the sarcophagus and aimed a kick at the lid. Bits of broken glass fell on the face and hands of the corpse and damaged it in several places, including the right eyebrow. The mausoleum was closed until 15 October for repairs. After this incident reinforced glass was used for the lid of the sarcophagus.

1 September 1973. A man smuggled a bomb into the mausoleum under his coat. It exploded near the sarcophagus, killing a couple of visitors from Astrakhan and injuring four schoolchildren. Lenin's corpse was unharmed. The terrorist was sent to prison for ten years.

1 November 1987. According to an account by V. Kamennykh, commanding officer of the mausoleum at the time, an unknown person threw a Molotov cocktail on to the sarcophagus, which did not catch fire.

28 April 1990. Another Molotov cocktail. The resulting fire was quickly brought under control.

1995. An unknown person threw an iron gearwheel on to the glass over the sarcophagus, although it did not do any damage. A medical examination showed that the would-be attacker was insane.

34. Gulag – acronym of the Russian words for Chief Administration for Corrective Labour Camps, a department of the secret police established in 1930.

35. Tupolev (1888–1972) suffered official disfavour from 1938–43, and spent some time in a labour camp. Responsible for the design of more than 100 military and civil aircraft, including the widely used TU-2 and TU-4 bombers of the Second World War, he also designed the first jet airliner and the first supersonic passenger aircraft to enter service. He was "rehabilitated" in the 1960s.

36. N.I. Yezhov replaced Yagoda as chief of the NKVD in September 1936, and headed it during Stalin's purges of 1936–8, a period which Russians referred to as "Yezhovshchina". Appointed to the Politburo in 1937, and made Commissar of Water Transport in 1938, he was dismissed as head of the NKVD later that year, on Stalin's orders. Arrested in 1939, he was executed in 1940.

37. Molotov had been appointed Commissar for Foreign Affairs in May 1939, and held the post until 1949, being reappointed on Stalin's death in 1953 until he fell foul of Khrushchev in 1956, after which he held only minor posts, and suffered periodic denouncement. He was eventually returned to favour, and died in 1986, aged ninety-six.

38. In 1949 this was renamed Humboldt University by the Soviets, since it fell within their sector. Former professors and students of the university established the Free University of Berlin in the Western Sector of the city.

39. This had been a continuing fear in those parts of Germany that lay in the path of the Red Army's advance during the last months of the war. In fact, it was partly inspired by Goebbels who, to stiffen resistance, warned that defeat by the Russians would lead the country being overrun by barbaric and ruthless Soviet Asiatics.

40. A.S. Abramov, *Lenin's Mausoleum*, Moscow, Moskovski Rabochi, 1972, pp.44–45 (in Russian).

41. Hermann Ludwig Ferdinand, Baron von Helmholtz (1821–94), German mathematician, physicist and physiologist, one of the formulators of the theory of the conservation of energy, inventor of the ophthalmoscope, and noted for his work on the physiology of the eye and ear.

42. Ivan Vladimirovich Michurin (1855–1935) was a Russian horticulturalist renowned for his breeding of new varieties of fruit and berries. His theory of cross-breeding, which put forward the idea that acquired characteristics can be inherited, was adopted as official state doctrine in the Soviet Union, and heavily influenced Lysenko in his anti-Mendelian theories.

43. For the Jewish Anti-Fascist Committee, see *Le livre noir* ("The Black Book"), Arles, Solin/Actes Sud, 1995, and *Prisonniers du pharaon rouge* ("Prisoners of the Red Pharaoh"), Arles, Solin/Actes Sud, 1997.

44. Bulgaria formed part of the Ottoman Empire for some 500 years, only becoming an independent kingdom in 1908.

45. Fighter escorts provided by the US Air Force, since the Americans had dominance in the air over North Vietnam. The logistics of the flight must have required considerable negotiation between the Soviet authorities, the North Vietnamese, and the US military forces.

46. What was to become Vietnam formed part of French Indochina from the 1880s until 1954.

47. It was in Yekaterinburg that Tsar Nicholas II and his family were murdered by Bolsheviks in July 1918.

48. *Argumenty i Fakty*, October 1993, no.40 (573).

Photographic Credits